The Home Kids

A social history of a Yorkshire family

1928 to 2018

Cover Photograph

The cover photograph is of Alice and George Gray taken c1935 outside their terraced house at 11 Paradise Place Hull.

The Home Kids

'The Home Kids' was the derogatory term used by some of the families living in Cottingham when referring to the boys living in the children's home at 17 Northgate.

The names of the boys and girls living in the children's home between 1944 and 1954 are fictitious to preserve anonymity.

All rights reserved. No part of this publication may be reproduced, stored in a retrieval system or transmitted in any form or by any means without the prior consent of the author, or be otherwise circulated in any form of binding or cover other than that in which it is published and without a similar condition being imposed on the subsequent purchaser.

All photographs are the property of the author, except the photograph on page 5 which is the property of Hull City Archives and Records Office.

Printed in the United Kingdom

Published by Fred Gray

Table of Content

Dedication
Foreword
Author

Acknowledgements

Part 1.

Chapter 1. The Gray Family …………………………………………....1

Chapter 2. Withernsea. 1940 - 1944 …………………………….....6

Chapter 3. Patrington. The Workhouse. ……………....................15

Chapter 4. The Cottingham Years 1944 - 1952…………………....18

Part 2.

Chapter 5. Starting a New Life …………………………………….....34

Chapter 6. June, George, Sally, John (Jack), James, Freda……………41

Part 3.

Chapter 7. The Lockwood Family
Sandra, Michael, Tom and Graham……………………………………54

Chapter 8   George Frederick Gray (Dad)……………………..66

Epilogue……………………………………………………………….68

Appendices……………………………………………………………70

Dedicated

To

"Our Mam"

Rose May Lockwood

1909 – 1987

A mother who suffered an horrific life-changing accident as a child which left her scarred for life. She lost her first family when they were taken into care in 1944 never to live together again. Her legacy is seven sons, four daughters, and over one hundred and thirty grand and great-grandchildren.

Foreword

This is the history of two families, both with the same mother but different fathers. It is a collection of ingrained memories and conversations with my mother and my eldest sister June Elizabeth. We begin in 1912 when my mother suffered her life-changing accident and continues through the Second World War to the present day. It is a social history of the years between 1912 and 2018, which follows the fortunes of the eleven children born to my mother. The eldest daughter June was christened under my mother's maiden name of Lockwood. The following six children were christened under the name of Gray, with the last four again christened Lockwood.

Up to the start of the 2nd World War, the country was locked into the 'Great Depression' and life was very hard. This was followed by six long years of war and a further ten years of recovery from those two momentous events in the history of our country. My mother's experience of those years from the time of her accident was months of pain during the treatment of her injuries, several years in rehabilitation, low paid kitchen work, sexual abuse by one of her employer's family, years of physical abuse by my father, enduring poverty on a scale not understood by many people today, and the loss of five of her children, taken from her and put into care in 1944, never to live together again.

The introduction of the Welfare State eased the burden of poverty and by 1948 she had started a second family of three boys and a daughter. Although poverty still existed education and discipline improved with the return of the male teachers from duty during the war. It was still a struggle for her, and life was never easy. It was only after her second family had become self-sufficient that she began to have a decent life of her own. The strain during her life of poverty and childbearing had taken its toll and at the age of seventy-eight she passed away in the Hull General Hospital. She had been lovingly nursed by her first daughter June who was a nurse at the hospital. Her second family was at her bedside.

The Author

Born in 1935 at the height of the 'Great Depression' the author had a tough childhood which included a short time in a Victorian age workhouse, and six years in a children's home After his release from the home, he took up two apprenticeships, the first with a joiners and undertakers and the second with a furniture manufacturer. His National Service commitment was deferred until his apprenticeship was completed and, at the age of nineteen, he joined 299 Parachute Squadron Royal Engineers, a Territorial Army unit based in Hull, Yorkshire. By the time he was called up for his National Service, in 1956 he was already a trained parachutist and a semi-trained soldier. After basic training and two brutal selection courses, he joined 9 Parachute Squadron Royal Engineers. Soon after joining his unit he committed himself to a full army career and as a member of 3 Troop, he served five months in Cyprus and Jordan and took part in a major airborne exercise in Norway.

In September 1959 he met his wife to be, Betty Anne Whitman, and they married in March 1960. Their son James David was born in 1961, who would also serve a full army career with the Grenadier Guards. In 1961 he left Airborne Forces for three years' service in Malaya (later to become Malaysia) accompanied by his family. Whilst there he served in North Borneo and Thailand. He also completed a Small Arms Weapons Course and an advanced Watermanship Courses before returning to the United Kingdom 1964. He re-joined 9 Parachute Squadron as a Sergeant where he was further promoted to Staff Sergeant and served in Kenya, Aden, and Libya. He completed a Quartermaster Sergeant Instructors Course at the Military School of Engineering Chatham, and an Officer's Weapons Course at Hythe in Kent.

Posted to Germany in 1969 he successfully passed a Ski Instructor's Course and completed a Winter Warfare Course in the Hartz Mountains. In 1971 he was posted to Canada as a Bridging Instructor with the Canadian Officer Cadets at the Royal Canadian School of Engineering in British Columbia. On his return to Germany, he took up the post of Sergeant Major of a Royal Engineer squadron based in Hameln, home of the fabled Pied Piper. On leaving the Army in 1980 he became a Ministry of Defence Courier and in the twenty-one years with them travelled nine and half million miles by air and many more by road. He has settled in Hampshire with his wife and their son, James David, who is married and has three boys living close by.

Acknowledgements

I would like to express my sincere gratitude to my old friend John Roberts BA (hons) MSc. A poet and author, who gave me advice and encouragement while preparing this book.

To Dr Gay Ecclestone, Mrs Ann Mogg and Mr & Mrs Steven McCarthy for the hours they spent reading and correcting the grammar and text, to ensure this family history is more readable than it would otherwise have been.

To Mr. Matt Eastell, for his patience and assistance in bringing this project to a successful conclusion.

Last but not least, to my wonderful wife Betty for her love and patience. Her knowledge of computers and constant encouragement helped me complete this two-year project.

Part One

Chapter 1

The Gray Family 1928 - 2018

My Mother, Rose May, was the youngest of three sisters and one brother born to John William Lockwood and Sarah Ann Bloom, on 26 May 1909. As I grew older, I became more aware of my surroundings and my family. I noticed that my mother had very bad scars on the lower part of her face, and the thumb on her right hand was bent so that the nail was almost touching the skin. I learned years later that she had been looking up the chimney for Father Christmas in her parents' house in Queen's Place, William Street Sculcoates, a district of Hull, when her life-changing accident occurred. She was only three years old at the time and her nightdress caught fire from an unguarded coal fire. She was severely burnt over her chest, arms and face and was to spend many years in hospital and in rehabilitation.

She had been taken to London for specialist care in one of the largest burn's units in Britain. I was well into my forties when she told me of her experiences in hospital and the excruciating pain of having her dressings changed every day, the memory of which haunted her for the remainder of her life. One pleasant event she never forgot was the visit of Queen Mary to the sick children's ward. The Queen stopped by her bed and spoke to her asking the usual questions. It was a memory she treasured always. During her years in the rehabilitation centre, she became very adept at making wax flowers from melted candles and small twigs, collected from the trees and bushes in the area where she lived. She was unable to knit because of her disability but was able to crochet. These were her only skills as she did not receive any formal education. She found work as a kitchen maid with a wealthy family in Kingston Surrey, but with the lack of education, no experience of life and without her parents to guide her she was totally unprepared for the outside world and its pitfalls. Someone took advantage of her innocence and made her pregnant with my half-sister June Elizabeth, the first of her eleven children.

My Aunt Nora insisted that the father was a travelling salesman, but Nora lived over two hundred miles away in Hull still living with her parents and was only eleven years old herself. It is unlikely she would know such details as who made her sister pregnant. My mother said it was the son of the family she was employed by. I think this is more plausible than the travelling salesman version. Within a few weeks, my mother was on the train back to Hull with her newborn daughter. It is probable that the family didn't want any scandal and packed her off to her own family, paying the fare as she would not have been able to afford it herself. There is no family record of where she lived on her return to Hull in 1928, possibly with her parents but during the next two years, she was to meet my father George Frederick Gray.

After leaving the army my father settled in Hull sometime between 1924 -25 with no skills and no pension. His future must have seemed bleak particularly with the Great Depression of 1929 on the horizon. At the age of twenty-eight, living on his own, he was without the umbrella of either his family or the army and had only manual labour as his job prospects. Life must have been very difficult, but it would appear he did not consider re-joining the army. He did have a trial for Hull City Football Club but his hopes of a career in football were dashed when his right knee was found to be too weak. This could have been the result of a gunshot wound to his right thigh suffered during the 2nd Battle of the Somme in 1918. Between 1928 and 1930 he met my mother and they set up home in Grey Street. It was there my eldest brother George William was born on the 5$^{th\ of}$ November 1930. Conditions at that time were quite reasonable and a photograph of the time shows June and George, very well dressed and healthy, posing for a studio picture. My father had no love for June, as she was not his daughter and she was terrified of him, especially when he removed his belt from around his waist to beat her if she had misbehaved, real or imagined. I have no memories of any mistreatment from my father during the five years I lived with him but on occasions, he did frighten me when he threatened to take me to the doctors, where he said they would lay me on a table and cut my stomach open to see why I wouldn't eat eggs!

The family moved from Grey Street to Paradise Place in 1932. Alice was born there in 1933 and I followed two years later in 1935. In 1936 we moved to 57 Lister Street, a basement house, and John David (Jack) was born there in 1937. He shared the same birthday as mam, 26th May. Our home in Paradise Place did not live up to its name and could only be described as a hovel. There were no indoor facilities such as water or electricity, very little in the way of furniture and a meagre amount of money to clothe, feed us and pay the rent. Life was a constant struggle for my parents and very unpleasant for us children. If we had coal, then a warm pleasant glow would come from the fire and my parents would sit either side of the grate on the only two chairs we had. I can remember the small reddish marks on my mother's legs as she sat too close to the fire and Cockroaches ran freely around the room and appeared to be part of normal life.

The house had two bedrooms, one for mam and dad and the other for five of us sleeping in one bed. The stairs were completely covered in with a door at the top and bottom. Because it was so dark on the stairs, dad (as a punishment) would lock us in on the stairs in the pitch black until he decided it was long enough. This was a punishment he used regularly. The only light in the house came from a suspended gas mantle in the front room. Gas flow was controlled by a meter, which required money inserted into the slot before gas was made available. There were no lights in any other rooms only paraffin lamps or candles. There was no water system in the house so when it was bath night the water, drawn from an outside tap, was heated in a very large kettle suspended over the fire in the front room. The bath was a tin-tub which, when not in use, hung outside on a wall in the back yard. We all used the same water and if the money and the coal had run out, bath night went by the board. We were lucky to have a bath once a week. There were public baths in the district for adults to use but these came at a price. The little money available was spent on food and rent after my father had taken his share for beer and cigarettes.

When it was time for us to go to bed, we climbed the stairs with June carrying a lighted candle in a saucer. Old coats for extra warmth covered us and June would tell us stories until we dropped off to sleep. We did not have any toys or teddy bears of any description; they were a luxury beyond our reach. On many occasions, my drunken father, beating our mam would keep us awake and we would lie silently listening to her crying and begging him to stop. Our playground was the Jewish burial ground just across the road from the entrance to our terrace. Here we could play hide and seek amongst the gravestones and feel grass beneath our feet instead of paving stones and cobbled streets.

Not far from where we lived there was a slaughterhouse where we could watch the animals being taken inside for slaughter to provide food for a very hungry population. The pier head was a short distance away from where we would spend hours watching the Humber Ferry arrive from Immingham and New Holland and the heavily laden barges ferrying goods from the docks to warehouses on the banks of the River Hull, a tributary of the Humber, which was also the eastern boundary of the city. We also liked to watch the large carthorses being washed down after their days work hauling the cargo from barges tied up alongside the banks of the River Hull.

Children had to make their own entertainment and the popular games at that time were Marbles, Hopscotch, a cigarette game called Flick, and Hide and Seek. Girls would practice handstands against any wall and 'skipping' if there was a rope available. One memory I have of Paradise Place was being cut on the head by either Alice or June when they were doing handstands against a wall. I must have been too close to whoever it was, and I was kicked in the forehead as she came down to a standing position. It must have been quite a cut as my father carried me to the Hull Infirmary to have it attended to.

When vegetables were available from my father's allotment, my mother would make a wonderful dumpling stew, it was one of the few things she excelled at. She had been taught how to make it when she was in service with the family in Kingston. In later conversations with June, I said I could never remember sitting down at a table to eat our meals. She said 'no, we stood at the table eating our bread and jam and sharing a mug of cocoa'. Money was so short that most children would be sent out onto the streets to pick up cigarette ends from the gutter where other smokers had thrown them. This practice was commonly known as 'tab-ending.' When we had collected enough our dad would take the small amount of tobacco left in the discarded tab end and roll it in a paper to make a very thin cigarette.

We moved from our slum houses on several occasions and this was called 'flitting.' It was either because my parents had fallen behind with the rent or the house had become inhabitable. With so little in the way of possessions only a small handcart was needed to move to our new lodgings. Everything we had was piled on the cart, and my father pulled it with the family walking behind. Only short distances were involved and usually only to the next street or terrace. We never moved far from where I was born. Dad had been out of work for  most of the 'Depression' but occasionally did find work as a labourer doing odd jobs. A small welfare handout from local charities was the only income to support a family of six. He had an allotment from which vegetables were available at the end of the growing season and they supplemented our diet of bread and jam. Our grandparents lived near Paradise Place and grandfather Lockwood delivered coal to the local area. The only memory I have of him was one day I ran out of the terrace and jumped up on the coal cart being pulled by a sorry looking horse. Other than that, I have no memory of him at all. Grandfather John William Lockwood was the son of John Barley and Sara Lockwood who were not married at the time. Years later I found out how John Lockwood's father was named John Barley Lockwood (as it appeared on the marriage certificate). His son John Thomas was born out of wedlock to Sarah Lockwood in 1871 and by law, he had to be baptised in his mother's maiden name. She lived with John Barley as his servant as it was illegal at that time for any unmarried couples to live together.

In 1874 John Barley and Sarah Lockwood married and John was re-christened, John William Barley. For some unknown reason, he had changed his middle name to William. John William moved to Hull where he met Emily Ann Bloom and they married in 1894 in the district of Sculcoates. By law, he had to be married in his birth name of John Lockwood. His father was recorded as John Barley Lockwood. The appellant had, by law, added the birth name of Lockwood to the name of John Barley (his father) creating the name of John Barley Lockwood a person who didn't exist.

Paradise Place during the slum clearances in the city of Hull in the fifties. My birthplace (number 11) had already been demolished a few years earlier.

Chapter 2

Withernsea

1940 - 1944

From the novel 'Aftermath' by Peter Robinson.

There are many English resorts that look as if they have seen better days. Withernsea looked as if had never seen any good days at all. The sun was shining over the rest of the Island, but you wouldn't know it at Withernsea. A vicious icy rain slanted in from the iron sky, the waves from the North Sea the colour of stained underwear churned up dirty sand and pebbles on the beach. Set back from the front was a strip of gift shops, amusement arcades, and a bingo hall, their bright coloured lights garish and lurid in the gloomy afternoon, the bingo caller's 'number nine, doctors orders' pathetic as it sounded along the deserted promenade

After weeks of living in fear of the nightly bombing of Hull, Withernsea in comparison was paradise. The beaches, the cliff tops, the sea, the amusement arcades, the cinemas, the orchards and the wide-open countryside with lots of wooded areas, rich in blackberries in August and September. It was ours to enjoy and keep us occupied during the summer months. The town was originally built as a resort for the citizens of Hull and the surrounding villages of the Holderness Plain. For the expected influx of visitors during the summer months, a railway line was laid from Hull to Withernsea in 1854. The town did become very popular with its clean air, beaches, a pier, a broad promenade, and a Convalescence Hospital for the elderly and infirm. People flocked to the town and it became quite prosperous in the early twentieth century. The other landmark of any significance was the inland lighthouse on Hull Road which was still in use during the 2nd World War. After its closure in 1966, it became a museum dedicated to the life of Kay Kendal, a famous actress and film star born in Withernsea.

My memories of moving from Hull to Withernsea are vague, but we must have travelled on the train or bus for about an hour. I can only estimate the year was late 1940-1941. The distance from the station to our house was about half a mile. It must have been a sorry sight to see a drably dressed woman with four children in tow, walking down the street of their town, refugees from the bombing of Hull. When we arrived at the house as it was getting dark and whoever was responsible for us had lit a fire. Candles produced a weak light in what was the middle room of the house, otherwise all I can remember is sitting on the floor in front of the fire eating bread and treacle. One way my mother managed to get some extra money was to sell our clothing coupons to the wealthier people of Withernsea as they were of little use to her. Spending money on clothing wasn't an option. With so little, our mam could not afford to feed us properly and we would often go hungry. I can't remember ever sitting around a table having a meal together. There was a fish and chip shop directly opposite our house and if it had been open the previous evening, I would be sent over in the morning to beg for some left-over cold chips, which mam would try to heat up on the weak flame of the gas ring. Sometimes we would have bread and jam and at other times nothing at all. In the summer we would take fruit from the orchards scattered around the countryside, and carrots, turnips and anything else we could lay our hands on from the farmlands. Our mam must have had food coupons as we did have bread and jam or treacle but that was all, never any luxuries such as cake or biscuits.

I remember one occasion during the winter, mam sent me to the shop to get a loaf of bread with the coupons. I was aware of people looking at me, dressed as I was and I felt ashamed of how I looked, dirty, with clothing that had not been washed for weeks and totally inadequate for the weather. I was in my usual clothes (winter or summer they were the same). I saw people looking at me, either in pity or horror I don't know, but I do remember saying to them 'my mother is going to make me wear my wellingtons when I get home' I might as well have said the Crown Jewels, as a pair of wellingtons were as much out of the questions as the jewels.

I'm sure the same people knew the Gray family and how they lived. We were probably the biggest problem family in town and certainly the poorest. My clothing consisted of a pair of short trousers, a jersey with two buttons at the collar, a pair of beach sandals, no underwear and certainly no coat, not even in the harsh weather that lashes the Withernsea coast in the winter months. Because of the inferior quality of the material, the buckle holding the strap of my sandals in place soon came off leaving the strap flapping around being of no use whatsoever. We did not have a change of clothing but during the summer months that was not too much of a problem as we spent most of our time in the sea. We didn't bother to take our clothes off; we just went straight into the water. If there was no one on the beach, then we went in naked and dried off naturally. I cannot remember how we washed in the winter as we had no indoor facilities so I can only assume we had a large bowl so our mam could wash us down standing in the cold kitchen.

Head lice were always present. Our hair was full of them and mam used a steel comb to rake through our hair. Hundreds of lice fell out on to the paper on the table then they were flushed down the lavatory if it wasn't frozen up.

During the summer months, my brothers and I spent most of our time either on the beach or playing around the seafront. We knew nothing of what was happening in the war except to watch the red sky over Hull after the nightly bombing raids by the Germans and that, the promenade had been put out of bounds to everyone by covering the whole area with barbed wire. Large blocks of concrete had been placed along the base of the cliffs and along the beach in the forlorn hope, they would stop enemy tanks getting ashore in the expected invasion. Pillboxes had been built into the steep side of the promenade, which could house one small gun and was also used by the sentry on duty to spot any occurrences that might indicate the invasion was imminent. A watchtower had been built on top of the twin towers of what was the entrance to the Victorian pleasure pier, destroyed when a cargo ship smashed into it during a storm in 1890.

Some days we could see smoke from the convoys of ships passing Withernsea out on the horizon. At the time we didn't know that some of those ships would be sunk and the debris would be washed up on the beach about two miles north of Withernsea. It was a peculiarity of the tide that swept the debris on to that part of the shoreline, but it would provide scavengers such as us, with driftwood to collect and chop into bundles to sell around the houses of the town. This was our main source of pocket money for our entrance fee for the local cinema and a bag of chips. Despite the conditions we were living under, the summer months were happy days for me. I was supposed to attend the infant's school but most of the time, I played truant. With Jack and my youngest brother Jim we ran wild and enjoyed the freedom of the beach and seafront, ignoring the warnings (we couldn't read them anyway). June attended the Withernsea High School until she was fifteen when she left to find employment helping my mother with the money problems. I remember very little about my sister Alice. After she was evacuated to Lincolnshire with George, I did not see her again until 1947 at the wedding of my eldest sister June to William Hare. By this time, she had found employment as a companion to a wealthy lady living in Brentwood Essex. She continued in this employment until the lady died years later.

When George came home to Withernsea he soon started to have problems at school. Since early childhood, he had suffered from poor eyesight and wore glasses of very inferior quality. He had great difficulty in seeing the blackboard in the classroom and his teachers had no understanding of his problem and often resorted to punching him in the back or giving him raps of the cane because of his poor work. It did not take long for George to rebel and refuse to go to school at all. His education, or lack of it, and poor eyesight was to be a great problem for the remainder of his life. Even as a five-year-old, straight lines and uniformity fascinated me. George would make me several aeroplanes out of kindling wood, simply by using one piece of wood as the fuselage, nailing a second and third piece across the first piece as the wings and tail wing. He would make me quite a lot of these and I would take great pleasure in lining them up in straight lines. These were my toys and I loved them. If anyone or anything annoyed him, he would smash the whole lot up by stamping on them but shortly after his outburst he would relent and make them again.

In the early months of 1944, the Army had arrived in Withernsea. The train from Hull pulled into the station and hundreds of soldiers spilled out on to the platform. To me, it was the most exciting thing I had ever seen as they formed up and with their regimental band leading. They marched off to their billets, some to a house almost opposite to the one we were living in and more on the corner of Alma Street. The soldiers in the house on the corner of Alma Street put a poster in the window of their billet and this also attracted my attention. I looked at it many times, never really understanding what it was all about. The poster depicted a red background with what looked like a city on fire. A person, wearing a cap and in uniform was on the right and on the left a woman, wearing a shawl and carrying a baby in her arms. The red glow over the city was easily identified because from the downstairs middle room of our house I had often watched the bright red glow in the sky as my hometown of Hull was on fire after the nightly bombing raids. I now know that the poster was depicting Hitler, the man in the uniform, watching the continent of Europe burning.

Alma Street was named after the 'Battle of the Alma' and a pub stood on the corner of Queen Street and Alma Street. The pub had a great fascination for me, not for what it sold but the magnificent sign that hung from a bracket on the wall. It depicted a scene from the battle of the 'River Alma' the famous painting of the 'Thin Red Line' I knew nothing of the history of the painting, it was the colour and the soldiers of the 93rd Highlanders repulsing the Russian cavalry during the Crimean War. I would never tire of looking at the painting and was very disappointed years later to find it had been replaced with a more modern sign which conveyed nothing of the original, which has now disappeared.

In the next few days, more soldiers arrived in the town but this time with tanks and Bren-Gun-Carriers. This was a dream come true. The huge tanks were parked at the top of Queen Street close to the cliff tops. We would stand and watch in wonder as the smaller tracked vehicles screamed up the side streets and did a left turn at speed tearing up the road surface as they shot off to the cliff tops. We listened to the band playing and hung around the soldiers billeted across the road from our house hoping for a handout and we were soon eating as much bread and jam as we could manage. Two of the soldiers became friendly with our family and soon started to bring food to the house. We christened them 'Blondie and Darkie'. One of them could well have been a medical orderly for when my youngest brother Jim developed a rash all over his body and one of the two, I don't know which, laid him on the table and covered his skin with a white powder or ointment. Medical treatment had to be paid for, so my mother was unable to afford any help from the local medical services.

Despite being hungry and badly dressed the cinema was our top priority. There were two cinemas in the town, next to each other. 'Big Kinema and Little Kinema' Our favourite was 'Little Kinema'. This one seemed to show the most popular black and white films with the heroes of the day, Roy Rogers and his horse 'Trigger', Gene Autry and Tonto, Tom Mix, and our all-time hero, Jonny Weissmuller as Tarzan. We did not have pocket money so other means had to be found to raise the necessary cash for entry. Sixpence was the price for children and a shilling for adults. Our best method of raising money was to sell bundles of firewood. First, we had to find the wood, which came from driftwood on the beach or taking it from underneath holiday caravans parked on a site not far from where we lived. George chopped the wood into thin pieces about six to eight inches long, tied them into bundles and then we then took them around the houses and sold them at three pennies a bundle. At the time, coal fires heated most of the houses and only the very wealthy could afford other means of heating their homes. The bundles were sold very easily as most people seemed to like having ready chopped wood instead of having to do it themselves.

In the brambling (wild blackberries) season my brothers and I would walk to the nearest woods and collect as many berries as we could. We used jam jars and any other containers we could find to carry them back home. Blackberries were plentiful as Withernsea had several large wooded areas within walking distance. We also had a regular customer, a lady who had a small shop close to where we lived. She paid sixpence for each jar. If berries were out of season and we hadn't managed to find any wood, then we would stand outside the cinema and beg. Our usual tactic was to say to any passer-by 'give us apny (half a penny) mister to get in' It worked well, and it wasn't too long before we had our money to get in. The next problem was that children had to be accompanied by an adult, except for Saturday morning. The last person who had made up our sixpence would then be asked 'will you take us in mister'. As soon as we were inside the adult would say, right clear off to the front and keep quiet'.

The first rows were for the kids and it was bedlam down there. When our hero appeared on the screen the noise was enough to raise the roof, jumping up and down waving arms, even fighting. Through the haze of cigarette smoke, the noise was added to by the adults shouting to the unruly mob at the front to 'sit down and shut up.' Not that the kids took any notice of them. The show was continuous so there was a constant changing of seats. As the latest people and kids came in there was a hunt for a vacant seat. When people stood up to leave, their seat would tilt back to the vertical position with a loud sharp clap and the same for putting the seat down. The front rows where the kids were sitting were the worst offenders, as they made no effort to adjust the seats quietly. Often fights broke out over who had the right to a vacant seat. It was only when the usherettes came down and threatened to throw some of the worst offenders out of the cinema that the noise quietened down for a while My brother George had broken his glasses and was reduced to an eyepiece like a monocle.

The glass was broken into two pieces and they often fell out onto the floor. George would force me to get down under the seat and search for the two bits of glass. When I had found them, he would replace them in the 'monocle' and put it up to his eye and watch the film until the next time the glass fell apart, which was often. If the film had been starring one of our favourite cowboys, after the show we would gallop down Queen Street slapping our backsides with a hand imitating our heroes as they chased the baddies in the film. Our next aim was to find more money to see the film over again the following day. Even though we were dressed in the barest of clothing and were always hungry, the cinema was our top priority.

One day when I was begging outside the cinema with my best friend Tony Bridlin. I had almost reached my target of sixpence when two soldiers came along heading for the cinema. I asked for the halfpenny which I needed to make up my entrance money. I could not believe my luck when one of them gave me sixpence. I didn't give my friend a second thought as I headed for the door with the two soldiers. After the show, I rounded the day off by treating myself to a bag of chips which I ate as I walked down the street back to our hovel.

On one occasion, I was out with George collecting firewood to sell. We saw some wood under a caravan and immediately relieved the owner of his property. On the way home, we were carrying a rather heavy piece of wood between us. At the end I was carrying, there was a large rusty nail, which I had not noticed. As the wood became heavier, I could not hold my end and I let it slip. The nail tore a large gash in my right thumb. When we reached home, I showed the gash to my mother and her immediate reaction was to cover her mouth with her hand and turn away to avoid seeing the blood gushing from my torn thumb. She told me to go outside and put my hand under the cold-water tap, which helped stem the flow of blood. I wrapped something around it, I have no idea what, but it did stem the flow of blood. I didn't have any medical treatment and there was no infection. It healed on its own and the scar is still visible seventy years later.

Anything that required a doctor's service had to be paid for. There was no National Health Service in those days. Another time, I needed medical attention for my head, after being pushed onto the railway line at the station as we waited for a train to arrive. Without warning, I was pushed on to the tracks by one of the Crane brothers who were not our best friends. He pushed with such force I fell and split my head open causing a large gash. I picked myself up and ran all the way home with blood pouring from my head. When my mother saw me, she couldn't face the sight of blood and told me to go to the doctor's house, which was not far from the station where I had just come from. I did receive treatment but have no idea who paid for it. I dreaded the thought of school and at every opportunity, I would be off to the sanctuary of the beach away from that awful smell of the classroom. My mother would drag me to the school gate with me crying and trying to pull away from her. As soon as she let go of my hand, I was off. In the end, she just gave up.

One day as I was leaving the house to go to the beach (I was playing truant again) I looked across the road and saw the headmaster of the infant's school. I immediately made a dash for the cliff tops. He chased after me on his bicycle, but I was too fast for him and when I reached the cliff I slid and tumbled down onto the beach. The headmaster followed me down leaving his bike at the top. Both of us were running as fast as possible, me to escape, the headmaster trying to catch a six-year-old delinquent who should have been at school. I won, he gave up the chase, but I still had to face him the next day. The cane was the usual punishment and I knew what was in store for me. I told George about the problem and said I wanted to kill myself. George, being the caring, helpful brother, he was said he would help me. He mixed a cup of powdered dye, used for colouring clothes and told me to drink it, which I did. It came to nothing, it only made me sick. I did go to school and take my punishment and thought that was the end of it, but not George.

A few days later I was standing on the cliff tops when he came up behind me and hit me with something and I fell over the edge. I tumbled down the cliff face which wasn't very steep, but at the bottom were coils of barbed wire put there as an anti-invasion measure. I was sliding down in a gully and when I reached the bottom, I slid straight under the wire emerging without a scratch. When I asked George why he did it he replied 'I thought you still wanted to kill yourself.' Who needed enemies like the Crane boys when I had George for a brother!

On the north promenade, a pillbox had been built into the steep concrete surface. Always an attraction for mischievous kids it wasn't long before someone fell in through the only entrance, a hole in the roof. It was me!! I can't remember how I came to fall but George climbed down into the unmanned pillbox and, putting me on his back, he climbed back out. I was convinced it was dark but later he told me it was daylight. I can only assume I had cracked my head and was suffering from a mild concussion. George took care of me showing once again his caring side from his usual bullying self. I don't know where or how it came about but one day we all had some new clothes, not new as bought in a shop but new as donated by some kindly person or charity. We were still making our picture money selling firewood. With George in charge, we walked to Sand-Le-Mere, a small village perched on the cliff tops about two miles north of Withernsea. For some reason, unknown to us at that time, there was always plenty of driftwood on the beach washed up by the tide from ships which been sunk in the North Sea. It was just a peculiarity of the tide in that area which made such rich pickings for scavengers like us.

After a long slog to the beach, we collected as much as we could carry and started our walk back to Withernsea. As George had suggested we walk along the beach there was no argument from the rest of us. What he did not consider was the tide! It was coming in fast and there was every possibility we would be trapped on the beach. We had to find a place to climb the cliff, which turned out to be more difficult as it started to rain making the cliff slippery and difficult to climb. We tried various places, but it proved impossible to get to the top with all our driftwood, so it had to be abandoned.

We eventually reached the top covered in mud from head to foot. George was not pleased, and his temper was rising as we blamed him for making us walk along the beach instead of the cliff tops. This made him even angrier and he threatened to push anyone else who complained back down the cliff. We believed him! We plodded on getting wetter and dirtier, with some of us crying with the cold. Nearing Withernsea we saw what appeared to be turnips in a field. To us hungry kids it looked like food so we each took one and by holding them against our stomach with both hands we added to the already filthy clay covering our jerseys, which up to a few hours ago had been new and clean.

My poor mother could do nothing, she rarely got angry and never hit us, it was not in her nature. She was very upset at the state of our clothes as they were all we had. I don't know how she managed to get them clean, as there was no hot water only cold from the outside tap. I remember the four of us, George, myself, Jack, and Jim sitting round a miserable fire that barely threw out any heat watching the turnips in a pan perched on the fire. We had taken our clothes off and were sitting on the floor sharing a blanket wrapped around us. I don't remember if the turnips cooked but it was all we had to eat. The blanket was probably one, that my father had brought home when he suddenly turned up for a few days' leave. George and I were walking past 'Watts' the bakers on the corner of Young Street and Queen Street on our way to the amusement arcade. Just before the corner, a soldier appeared in front of us. He was in full uniform with packs on his back and carrying a rifle. He also wore a heavy full-length coat. I said to George 'that looks like dad', it was. He didn't say much but gave us a few pennies and told us to go to the amusements. This was the first time we had seen him since he was recalled to the Army at the beginning of the war. After a few days leave he returned to his unit and that was to be the last time I would see him until many years later when I saw him on Spring Bank Avenue in Hull around 1954. He had deserted our family and taken up with another woman whom I only knew as Ivy Sidebottom. He asked me to come to his house in Alexandra Terrace for dinner on the following Sunday and that's how I met him again.

It must have been my birthday after the soldiers had arrived in Withernsea. I asked my mother if I had any presents. 'No' was the answer, but I could have that bag of nuts and bolts I had been playing with for some time. (they were the nuts and bolts for the indoor shelter we had but never erected). I played in the front bedroom of the house, which was completely empty, no furniture and no carpets. The bolts were my soldiers and the nuts were the tanks. Now they were mine and I couldn't have been happier. I would line the bolts up in straight lines with a band at the front, the same as the soldiers had when they were on parade. The nuts and bolts were quite large and stood on the bare floorboards without constantly falling over. I also had a lot of cartridge cases, which I collected from the cliff-top area when the soldiers had finished their training. The spent bullets made ideal soldiers for my army. When my family was taken into care later in the year, I hid the cartridge cases under the tiles in the outdoor lavatory intending to recover them when I came back home. I never did, as I was not to return to Withernsea for a very long time.

By the middle of 1944, the situation for the family was deteriorating even further. We were already on the bottom rung of the ladder and ready to fall off. Of the four boys, only I attended the local infants' school but even that was spasmodically. In the summer my brothers and I would play in the pools by the breakwaters hunting for small crabs, which had no nutritional value, whatever. When we came out of the water, we let our bodies dry naturally. As an alternative, if the sea was too rough for swimming, we would go to the open-air swimming baths. They were opened in 1911 and were refilled on the turn of the tide with seawater being drawn in by a petrol-driven pump. It was always freezing cold, but we didn't care, at least it meant we were getting a bath of some sort during the summer months, otherwise, it can only be imagined what a state we would have been in had we not used the sea to wash.

I decided to join the local Cub Pack, as their hut was only a short distance from our house. The cub master must have been horrified when I appeared and asked to join. Only the lads from the better off families joined the Scouts and Cubs and I was not by any means in their league. When the cub pack was asked if they wanted me, there was a resounding 'No' and I was shown to the door. (so much for good deeds).

The Army left Withernsea as suddenly as it arrived a few weeks earlier. I had no idea where they had gone but it was the summer months of 1944. It could have been for the docks in Hull just sixteen miles away. Being too young to know anything about the war apart from the experience of the bombing of our city, and with hindsight, they were probably part of the D-Day invasion army. We left Withernsea shortly after their departure. Before they left Withernsea there was an incident that I have never forgotten. It was the bombing of Withernsea. I was on the beach with one of my brothers when it started to rain. We left the beach and took shelter in a hut, which was in the corner of the local Bowling Green. When the rain stopped, we decided to make a run for it and ran across the green towards the far-left side corner and up onto the road leading towards Queen Street. Only two or three minutes later a German aircraft flew over the town from the direction of the railway station. Before it reached the pier towers it dropped two bombs, one hitting a shop in the main street of the town killing seven people and the second one landed a few feet away from the hut where we had been sheltering a few minutes earlier. Two soldiers on the roof of the clubhouse were also killed. Just seconds before we reached Queen Street a man pushed us both into a shop doorway out of the path of any shrapnel coming our way.

Having reached rock bottom, I assume the local authorities had decided it was time for something to be done about the Gray family. The only money my mother had was a small allowance my father sent her and the few shillings my eldest sister June earned in the laundry of the workhouse. I cannot remember how we travelled to the Workhouse in Patrington, which was about five miles from Withernsea, but that is where we were to spend the next few weeks until George, Jack, Jim, Freda and myself would be sent to children's homes elsewhere in East Yorkshire.

Chapter 3
Patrington
The Workhouse

The workhouse was a staging post until a more permanent home could be found for the five us. June was sixteen years old and classed as an adult, so she stayed in Withernsea. We did see her on occasions when she came into the workhouse for her job in the laundry, but I have no recollection of Alice, she certainly was not with us at the time. The main building of the institution was built in 1837/8 and a hospital wing was added in 1902 which had four wards and two day rooms. Its purpose was to house the poor and destitute of Withernsea and the surrounding countryside. Patrington is a small rural farming town on the main rail and bus route between Hull and Withernsea.

Because it was built in a rural area it did not have the grim ugly appearance of other workhouses built in the cities and it had flowerbeds and a vegetable garden, which helped to feed the inmates. There was also a pigsty behind the main building. That part of the building to the right of the picture is the hospital wing where we had a room during our short stay in the institution. The main hall where we had our meals was a typical Victorian design with tables and benches down each side and more down the middle with a single table at the top end of the hall. The other end was where the Master and Matron controlled the issue of food and generally kept watch on the one hundred and fifty or more inmates. The tables were made of heavy wood without any type of covering, no doubt much easier for washing down after each meal. The benches were simply two planks with legs but no backrest. The walls were devoid of any decoration and the floor was made up of large rectangular flagstones. Again, this made it much easier for washing and cleaning. It was clear that workhouses were built to provide the minimum comfort for the inmates and not a place to linger too long.

One abiding memory I have of the meals and the other inmates was the drabness and the look of sadness on their faces. Most of the noise came from people scraping plates and the general noise created by a large gathering of people. The whole memory is of a grey mass of humanity. There was one man I have never been able to forget. He was sitting at the table at the back of the hall opposite where the Master and Matron were standing and only a few feet away from where we were sitting. He must have been mentally ill as he would cram bread into his mouth until he had a large ball hanging over his bottom lip and using his hand to hold it in place trying to chew it. He was one of those people who had a large head that made the spectacle even worse. It was a horrible sight and one I have never been able to forget. I can't remember what we had for breakfast, but I would think it would be a bowl of porridge with something to drink and the evening meal would be bread and soup. I cannot remember ever having anything at midday.

The Master and Matron had taken responsibility for our welfare, although my mother still looked after Freda who was less than two years old. George suffered the worst experience when he had to sleep in the men's dormitory. He kept threatening to run away if he had to continue sleeping in the same room as those men and he told me of his experiences. The old men were constantly coughing, snoring and wandering around the beds as though they were lost. The shuffling to and from the toilets went on throughout the night and mentally ill men whimpered and often would wake up crying from bad dreams. For a boy not yet fifteen years old, it must have been a nightmare. The threat of him running away didn't happen and he was moved to another room, possibly in the hospital wing.

George and I went to the village school, which was only a short distance from the institution. It had two classrooms and I remember I cried most of my first day. I could not understand anything the teacher was saying, as at that time I was totally illiterate, as was George. I don't think anyone cared whether we attended school or not but the pair of us were off into the countryside at every opportunity. The village of Patrington was situated in a beautiful part of the 'Holderness Plain' and had lots of wooded areas and farms. Ponds were plentiful and we would spend our day watching the Stickleback fish, the newts, butterflies, dragonflies and frogs. We were not able to catch anything as we had nothing to keep them in, but we did enjoy ourselves. We also searched the woods and hedges for birds' nests but as the nesting season had already passed, we found nothing but empty nests. Although we missed the cliffs, the beach, and the sea of Withernsea this was probably the happiest time of our young lives so far. Little did we realize this brief period of freedom was soon coming to an end. It was to be like a shutter closing out the sun.

June 27th 1944 started the same way as all the previous days. We had breakfast but after that, I cannot remember what happened to Jack, Jim and Freda. It was as though they just vanished, I was not to see them again until 1948. Later I did discover they had been taken to a children's home in Driffield. George and I followed later but we were taken to Cottingham, a village four miles north of Hull, reputed to be the largest village in England. My mother was not present when the person came for us and as with my three younger siblings, there were to be no goodbyes. We were separated and not told where we were going, or where each other had gone. It is possible that as we were being taken to separate locations it was best to avoid any last-minute scenes of distress. My mother was not there, and I assumed (correctly) she was kept away in another room for the same reason. It would probably have been too much for her to see her family being broken up and separated. Standing at the bus stop we did not have any luggage, as we had no possessions of our own, all we had was what we wore at the time.

Watching mam walk through the workhouse gate and walking to the bus stop and not waving to George and me as we waited with our escort, who never spoke any words of comfort to us or even smiled, I was completely bewildered as to what was happening and why were we waiting for a bus, and where were Jack, Jim and Freda. I was not aware that this day, twelve days after my ninth birthday, was to be the last time that we would ever be together again. My days of freedom were abruptly ended, and six years of discipline and restriction was about to start. When our mam walked through the institution gate and did not look at George and me across the road I now understand why. Years later she told me that she had been held in another room and was not allowed to say goodbye to us. She did see us at the bus stop but was so heartbroken she could not look back. She told me she cried every night for months after our separation. She was not a bad mother just not capable of caring for six children without enough money to feed and clothe them. Her parenting skills were poor and by the time we went into care she had lost control of the four boys. None of us were attending school and we were just running wild.

Chapter 4
The Cottingham Years
1944 - 1950

June 27th 1944 was the start of the breakup of the Gray family. I have very few memories of the start of the day, but my first recollection was being taken from Patrington to the village of Cottingham about four miles north of Hull. I clearly remember waiting at a bus stop with my brother George and a lady I had never seen before. As we waited, I saw our mother come through the gate of the workhouse and turn left walking towards the bus stop on the opposite side of the road. She was going back to Withernsea without any of her family and we had not been given the opportunity to say goodbye to her. She did not look back at George and me and that was to be the last time we would see her for the next four years. We had not said goodbye to Jack, Jim or Freda, they vanished from our lives until we met up again on a holiday at Withernsea in 1948. I have no idea how long the journey took but finally, we reached Cottingham and walked from the village square past the church of St Mary's and the Infant school on the opposite side of the road. We continued down a snicket (a paved path about four feet wide with hedges on either side) and crossed the Cottingham Beck (a small stream) and continued until we reached a gate that led into Northgate. We turned right and walked for a short distance until we came to number seventeen.

It was an ugly grey brick three-story house with a front garden and a path leading to the front door. A pleasant looking lady, who we came to know as 'Aunty Staves' opened the door and we entered into a spacious hall. George and I stood there waiting whilst our escort spoke to Mrs Staves and left without speaking or even looking at us, no doubt glad to be rid of two dirty smelly little boys. Mrs Staves must have been horrified at the state of my teeth as the first thing she did was to take me straight to the back scullery where there were two washbasins and several towels hanging on hooks on the wall. She gave me a toothbrush and showed me how to clean my teeth, which was a new experience for me as I could never remember cleaning my teeth before. We were given something to eat and drink and told to sit in what was the dining room for the occupants of the house, ten boys with similar backgrounds as ours.

After a brief time, George asked Mrs Staves if we could go outside for a walk. She said 'yes, but don't wander too far away, or you might get lost'. We turned right out of the gate and after a short distance from the house, we walked over the level crossing of the railway line for the train service between Bridlington, Beverly, Cottingham, and Hull. To the left of the crossing was a road, which ran parallel with the railway and out into the countryside with fields on both sides, a few smallholdings and the odd paddock with horses grazing. This was the road we were told to go down but George, ignoring those instructions, said quite unexpectedly 'I'm off- back home to Withernsea.' With that, he was gone. It was pure luck that we were on the road going to Hull, as we had no idea where we were. How he navigated around the city I will never understand, but he did and walked the twenty-four miles back home. I was left with having to tell a lie to Mrs. Staves, asking her if George had come back, knowing full well he hadn't. Poor Mrs Staves, by being nice to us and allowing us to go for a walk, had lost one of the children in her care within a few hours of our arrival. I was told to sit in the dining room and not to leave the house again. In the room, I saw what appeared to be open boxes piled in one of the alcoves near a large window. They were, in fact, the lockers belonging to the other boys who lived there and were still in school. There were twelve boxes each holding several books and other items. Being inquisitive I had a good look through each of the boxes in turn. I could not make sense of the books simply because I couldn't read, but I did enjoy the pictures. I had never seen books before, as they did not exist in my world, not even at the infant's school I had attended in Withernsea before being taken to the workhouse. After a while, I tired of the books and sat on one of the hard chairs and waited.

Later in the afternoon, there was a sudden commotion as the other children of the home arrived from school. They seemed to be a happy bunch with lots of shouting and laughing and greeting Aunty Staves as someone they were pleased to see. They all had their clothing inspected to see if any repairs and darning of socks were needed. Immediately the inspection was completed they changed into their working clothes. The older boys had an allotted task and they didn't appear to have to be told what to do. The house became a hive of activity and all I could do was watch and wonder what was going on.

I helped myself to a book from one of the lockers and settled down to look at the pictures again. Suddenly there was a high-pitched scream from one of the boys. He rushed over to me and tried to push me off the chair I was sitting on. It was Geoffrey Arnold and it was his locker from which I had taken the book. I didn't know this was the private property of the boys in the home. Geoffrey was a nasty character and I found out later he was the favourite of the matron, whom I had yet to meet. He was much older than me and much bigger so there was no way I was prepared to argue or explain myself as to why I had borrowed one of his books. I never did make friends with him and it was only a few months later he left, going back home to his parents.

That first night I was shown to the bed that was to be mine for the next six years and two months. It was in a corner of the front bedroom adjacent to a fireplace. Although most of my thoughts had been about my new surroundings, I became aware that for the first time in my life I was without any of my family. I was in a strange house with ten other boys of whom I did not even know their names. My mother was in Withernsea with my sister June, and I had no idea where Jack, Jim, and Freda had been taken. Alice was still with a family somewhere across the River Humber and George had deserted me for his own freedom. My father was with the Army, but I had no idea where. I didn't know why I was in this house or how long I was going to be there, I felt frightened and alone, I just wanted to go back home to be with my mam. Before our separation, I had given little thought to mam but now she was not there I missed her terribly. At the time I didn't know it was to be over four years before I was to see her again.

The next morning someone told me to get up and get dressed and I was shown how to make up my bed. My chair was placed at the bottom end, and the bedspread, blankets and sheets thrown over its back. After the mattress had been turned over, the sheets and two blankets were put back over the mattress and the edges were tucked in all around with the top sheet being turned back about twelve inches at the head. The bedspread was added, and perfect hospital corners were made at each end. After my brief instructions, I was told to sit on the bottom step of a flight of stairs leading to two attics above. As I sat there, I could hear all the hustle and bustle as the polishing and scrubbing went on with hardly a word being spoken. I had no idea what was to happen next, but I was soon to find out.

The bedroom door, just a few feet away from where I was sitting, opened and there stood the woman who was to rule my life for the next six years. She stood towering over me and said in a loud menacing voice "what's your name and where is your brother" To me, a skinny nine-year-old kid no more than four feet six inches tall she looked huge. Her arms would frighten any professional wrestler and she exuded hostility. There was no friendly welcome or pleasantry, which boded badly for my stay in this house. She told me to sit on the stairs and wait for breakfast to be called. With that Miss Duncumb, the Matron stormed off to inspect the work being done by the other lads. The frantic pace of upstairs before breakfast was now taking place downstairs. There were several jobs to be completed before breakfast and those with nothing to do washed and cleaned their teeth in the scullery washbasins before changing into their school clothes. When the polishing and scrubbing was complete, breakfast was called. We stood behind our allotted chairs with our hands clasped as in prayer to say Grace. The boys chanted 'For what we are about to receive may the Lord make us truly thankful, amen. I didn't know the Grace or what it even meant at that time, but we were being thankful for two cups of coffee and three slices of bread and dripping. After breakfast, the table was cleared and scrubbed, then dried off while someone swept the floor. The breakfast plates and cups were washed and returned to the crockery cupboard. When the clearing up was completed to Miss Duncumb's satisfaction, those not already in their school clothes could change and dash off to school hoping to beat the assembly bell.

Throughout my time in the home, the ritual never changed and nor did the bread and dripping. The exception was Sundays when we had a single boiled egg, but still with the bread and dripping. After this nutritious breakfast and everyone had eaten their bread, we stood behind our chairs and thanked the Lord for what we had received. Followed by the Lord's Prayer. On my first full day, after the other boys had left for school, I was given what were to be my school clothes: a shirt, pullover, a pair of short trousers, complete with braces, a jacket, a pair of long socks, and a pair of black leather lace-up boots. The trousers had six buttons on the waist, two on each side and two at the back. There were also four more buttons in the front, which had to be unfastened to put the trousers on or take them off. After putting on my new clothes Miss Duncumb took me to the Cottingham Primary School for Boys to be enrolled. Until I left six years later it was to be the only school I attended.

During the next few days, I was to learn the layout of my new home. On the top floor, there were two attics, one larger than the other. The second floor had four bedrooms, a lavatory, and a bathroom. The front bedroom (the largest) had eight beds, three situated to the right of the door and three to the left. Two more against the third wall, separated by a fireplace (it was never lit the whole time I lived there). The fourth wall had a large bay window with heavy curtains, which took up a third of the wall space. My bed was in a corner of the room next to the fireplace. The floor was bare boards painted gloss black. Each morning, except Sundays, the eight beds were pulled to the center of the room and whoever had that room to clean, first laid 'Ronuk' floor polish over the floorboards and when it had dried sufficiently was polished with a cloth. The beds were then pushed back to the wall and the centre of the room and polished in the same way. Between the front and back bedroom was a landing about thirty feet in length. It had a covering of brown linoleum and had to be polished the same way as the front bedroom. The back bedroom, which had four beds, also had a linoleum floor covering. Halfway down the landing was the 'isolation room' for any of the boys who might have a contagious health problem. I only saw it used twice and that was by two of the boys who occasionally returned to the home, especially during the war. One was Walter Williamson who had been wounded in North Africa, and the other a Royal Navy sailor Jim Oldfield.

The large ground floor, being the main living area, had six different areas. Two living rooms, a kitchen, pantry, scullery, and a back scullery. The largest of the living rooms was Miss Duncumb's sitting room and the second was the dining room and playroom for twelve boys. This room also had twelve lockers in one of the alcoves for private property. When we first arrived at the house there were ten boys, George and I made the number up to twelve, which was the capacity for the house. Two doors away there was a home for girls with the same number of occupants. I was to learn very quickly that fraternizing with the girls was strictly forbidden and if anyone was caught breaking the rules a few raps of the cane on their hands soon persuaded the culprit it was not a clever idea to go chasing after them. There was now a whole new set of rules for me to live by. The first rule was, I had no say in what I could wear, where I could go, when I went to bed and when I had to get up, what I ate, and that I was not allowed to leave anything I did not like, I could not go to the lavatory or leave the house without Miss Duncumb's permission and I had to attend church every Sunday morning for Matins, and Sunday school in the afternoon. After I had been compulsorily made a full member of the church (by Confirmation) I had also to attend Communion in the morning and Evensong in the evening. That meant three times to the church and Sunday School in the afternoon.

The second and worst rule was punishment. If you did anything wrong the rule was you had to be punished. This came in varying degrees. The easiest was losing our sweet ration, or being sent to bed straight after school, or being denied the pleasure of going to the cinema on a Saturday afternoon which happened maybe once a month in the summer (but not at all in the winter). The most feared was the cane. It looked like the short end of a snooker cue cut to a length of about three feet. For the unlucky one about to be caned Miss Duncumb would take hold of his wrist in a vice-like grip and with his fingers held out straight the cane was brought down with a vicious swish which produced the most agonizing pain. She would then take the other wrist and repeat the action. The number varied but the minimum was always three raps on each hand.

The worst I ever experienced was ten on each hand and that was for breaking the dining room window whilst playing cricket in the tiny back yard of the house. I had broken the window when she was away on her annual holiday and I had the agonizing wait for her return knowing full well what I was about to receive. I had never experienced pain like that and never did again in my lifetime. My hands felt as though they were on fire and no matter what I tried to ease the pain nothing alleviated that excruciating agony. One of the boys told me to put my hands in chilly water but that only made it worse. I put both hands underneath my armpit but that didn't help either. I could not help but cry and just wait for the pain to go away.

My punishment could be described as moderate compared to what some of the boys suffered. She seemed to get pleasure seeing their reaction as she brought down that vicious cane. One boy, Simon Metcalf, would jump at each stroke as though he was on a hot floor and could not escape. During my time in the home, I think he was abused in this way more than any other of the children and in addition, he was made to wear short trousers which were far too small for his large frame, tartan socks, and black lace-up boots. This made him a target of ridicule by other school children. He would often be seen standing with his back to a wall, crying with rage and his fists clenched as the kids tormented him. He could be calmed down by one of us from the Home calling him by his Christian name rather than just his surname. He didn't have any friends because of his temperament and was not a likable person but by treating him as a friend he could be calmed down. Three of the boys suffered more than the others. They were what today would be classed as special needs children. To us, they were just 'daft'. They were always being caned, for some reason or another and I do know that at least two of them were sent to 'institutions' after they left the home.

One of the easier punishments was being sent to bed early. This entailed the culprit having to go straight to bed following the inspection of his clothes after school. In the summer months going to bed at four-thirty meant changing into pajamas and lying in bed with the jacket buttoned up to the neck with nothing to do other than think. No books or radio were allowed in the bedrooms. Even conversation was not allowed once everyone had come up for the night. Laying there alone with the bright summer sun outside with curtains drawn and nothing to do, was to a child like a prisoner being thrown into an isolation cell. The offender came down for his tea, but it was straight back up after

Grace and the Lord's Prayer. This form of punishment could last a few days or even a few weeks. The work and repair jobs had to be done by one of the other boys, but they understood, as it happened to us all at one time or another. A simple punishment was for the offender to lose his 'sweet ration'. Every few weeks Miss Duncumb would open the top cupboard and hand out three boiled sweets kept in a large glass jar. It never occurred to me at the time but to have any sweets at all during the war years was a tremendous privilege, although there was a penalty. We had to give her a kiss on her stubbly face, a chore we hated more than anything else.

For those who had a job to do during the dinner hour they first had to don their working apron. These were like a butcher's apron, with a thinner stripe and they hung on a peg on the door of the under stairs' cupboard. Each had a number stitched on to identify the owner. Coal scuttles had to be refilled, and the table set for dinner. Once dinner was over the crockery, utensils and the pans used to cook the meal had to be washed and returned to their allotted place in the cupboards. At the same time, the table was washed and scrubbed, and the floor swept. It was back to school for the afternoon session until four o'clock and then home for clothing inspection and the jobs which had to be done before tea. A variety of work had kept most of the boys busy such as peeling the potatoes, carrots, and turnips, cleaning and polishing twelve pairs of boots, filling the coal scuttles, setting the table for tea, and cleaning and polishing every item in the cutlery box.

The dog, 'Gyp' was taken for his walk by the 'dog walker' and any errands to the grocer's shop in the village was undertaken by one of the lucky boys in favour at the time. These last two jobs were the most sought after as it gave a short period of relative freedom away from the house. Whilst these activities were keeping the older boys occupied the younger ones without any work to do would sit in the dining room and read their books or whatever they had in their personal locker box, waiting for the tea to be served. Tea was a simple meal lasting no more than fifteen to twenty minutes. The menu could be predicted and again it never changed. One night it would be a piece of 'Brawn' with three slices of bread. Another night it would be a piece of cheese with the bread. Our favourite was baked beans doled out with a ladle onto a plate. Sunday was the best tea as it usually had a cake of some description. Miss Duncumb was a good cook and one of our best-loved was Kellogg's corn flakes dipped in chocolate and left to solidify.

The downside to the Sunday tea was what we had to endure before we could sit down. 'Senna pods'!! Every alternate Sunday we were given a dose of this vile-smelling horrendous tasting laxative. Everyone dreaded it, but for two of the boys, Thomas Atkinson, and Terrance Bailey it was a nightmare, Terrance told me that just the thought of it made him feel ill with the anticipation of this ordeal and his fear of it started early in the morning. The two of them were made to stand at the sink where Miss Duncumb would stand behind them and beat the back of their legs with the cane to encourage them to drink. At each attempt to drink they would both throw up and their cup was refilled. The ordeal for them lasted a long time but in the end, they had to drink it to the last drop.

The result of this evil came during the early hours of the next morning. We were woken up by a desperate need to go to the lavatory. The main problem was that all twelve of us needed the lavatory at the same time. With only one upstairs and the other downstairs, it became a desperate wait to get into the toilet before a change of pyjamas was necessary. At least three or four visits were necessary before the effects of the laxative wore off. By the time we had to get out of bed everyone was exhausted from the lack of sleep, but the morning chores still had to be completed.

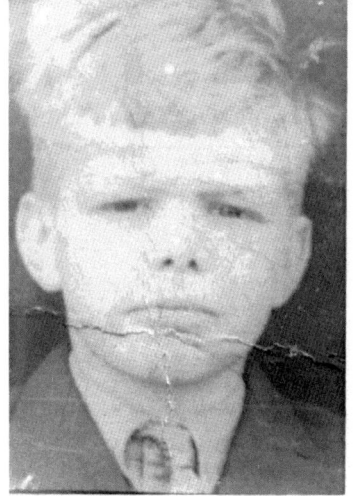

During the weekdays whilst we were having tea and if Miss Duncumb was in a good mood then we could listen to a radio programme 'Dick Barton Special Agent' on the wireless relay box mounted on the wall above the table. It was everyone's favourite and not one to miss. If she was not in a good mood or something had annoyed her, turning the relay box off was a way of collective punishment for us all. When tea was over the older boys would start the darning and mending. I can't remember what the routine for the little ones was. When it was bath night then they would certainly go straight to bed after drying and putting on their pyjamas.

The darning and repair of trousers and socks were done after tea, sitting in Miss Duncumb's room. We could listen to the radio as we worked in front of a blazing fire during the winter months, and in the kitchen or dining room in the summer. There was only one spare armchair in Miss Duncumb's room and that could be reserved by anyone of us. Uncomfortable upright hard chairs were for the rest of the group.

After a few months of training, I was the best at darning, so the job of darning her stockings fell to me for which she would pay me a pittance of three pence per hole. The holes were enormous, caused by whatever she used to keep them up and I would have to use a plate or saucer for me to be able to stretch the hole, as they were always too large for my hand. For this service, I automatically had the right to the armchair, especially if I was in favour. When all the repairing and darning was finished, we would play 'Rummy,' a card game she enjoyed just as much as we did. At 9 o'clock we went to bed.

The day-to-day routine rarely changed, and it depended very much on Miss Duncumb's mood. She had a volatile temperament with anger very close to the surface. She also played mind games often directed at an individual or all of us. During one of the periods I was out of favour she made my life more miserable than it normally was. My job was washing up after tea. After I had completed that, with everything back in the cupboards I had to wash the draining board down and scrub the tea cloth. After I had finished my chores in the kitchen, I had a wash in one of the washbasins in the scullery. Before I could dry myself, I had to follow the normal procedure, which was, whilst I was still wet to go through to her living room for inspection. First, I held the towel to show both sides followed by both arms, back and front and the same with my legs. After the inspection, I returned to the scullery and dried myself. I then returned to her room with my towel and showed her both sides. If it was dirty in any way it would attract a minor punishment. Once I finished my duties, I could join the others in the sitting room to start darning and any other repairs for my 'little one'.

The darning needles (six of them) were kept on a piece of cardboard with the owner's initials above each one. When I came to get mine, there was none left!! I told Miss Duncumb and she said, "find it". We all knew what she had done. Before anyone had started their darning, she had removed one needle. As each one of the others took the piece of cardboard and saw theirs was missing that person just took anyone that was left. This would be repeated until there was none left and that meant someone (me) had to search for a needle that was not really missing. I did ask if I could have the light on in the kitchen but that was refused. All I could do was to go into the kitchen, sit on a chair, feel sorry for myself for a while then go and ask her for a new needle, which she then gave me. That was her way of playing mind games.

One other way for me was through my love of football. In 1947 football was the passion of my life. It was the only team sport played by the school and I was good enough for the first eleven. My friend Trevor Ashton gave me a pair of his old soccer boots and a pair of shorts. That was my soccer kit. During the season the team played on Saturday mornings and for Miss Duncumb this was an opportunity to make my life just that little bit more difficult. A large black kitchen range had been installed and I was given the job of cleaning it every Saturday morning. It was a job that could last well over an hour and to make sure I would miss the start of the match she would give me additional jobs before I was told I could go. I raced along Northgate to the playing fields at the recreation ground, which took about ten to fifteen minutes. Invariably I was late and, on several occasions, someone else had taken my place.

The biggest disappointment that happened to me was the visit of a magician for the entertainment of the joint girls' and boys' homes. In the football season 1947 – 48 (by this time, I was twelve years old) the school team had fought its way to the semi-final of the Holderness Shield, the most prodigious event in the football calendar, a competition the school had never won. The date for the game was the same day as the visit of the magician. The joint number of the two homes was twenty-four with two matrons and two helpers, more than enough to fill the back yard of the house where the show was to take place. Miss Duncumb insisted I attend the show and miss the football match. I was totally devastated by this mean small-mindedness. The team won the semi-final and was to play Hornsea School in the final. Trevor had a great game in the semi and could not be dropped for the final, so I was made the first reserve. I was bitterly disappointed as the team went on to beat Hornsea five goals to nil. Trevor came up against the International schoolboy player Len Vickerton and had a terrific game, proving his selection was the correct one but very hard for me to accept. I have disliked magicians ever since and would walk ten miles to avoid one.

Laundry night was always on a Wednesday that for some reason never done not produce an atmosphere of tension. Possibly because for some of the lad's things came to light during the checking of trouser pockets and bedding. On one inspection a letter, intended for the local police, was found in the trouser pocket of Albert Crooks. It was a collective complaint about our treatment and especially the punishments. He was the writer, but it was signed by three others including myself. It was his brother who found it and not realizing what its content was handed it to Miss Duncumb. The house erupted with dire consequences for everyone. Instead of her lying in bed having had a cup of tea brought up to her by whoever was on breakfast duty, she was up before us and always in a foul temper. Everything was restricted and things, like going to the cinema on a Saturday and visiting friend's houses for tea, was stopped. We could not go to the recreation ground and had to stay and play in the tiny backyard of the house. She was clearly worried about the letter, but nothing came of it and gradually the routine returned to normal including the use of the cane.

Only once or twice did I ever see an inspector from County Hall, visit the home. After talking with Miss Duncumb in private we were assembled in one of the rooms and with Miss Duncumb standing close by, we were asked if we were happy and had anything to say. As Miss Duncumb stood there with a menacing look there were never any complaints!! The inspector would also look at the 'punishment book' and as far as I can remember there was never any comments about it. Bath night was once a week, which also brought on a bad mood in Miss Duncumb. Everyone would strip off their clothes and stand on the landing outside the bathroom. The first two would get into the bath and Miss Duncumb would wash the first one in about half a minute. He would jump out and collect his towel and dry himself. The next one in line would then get into the bath behind the one already there. There were always two in the bath except for the last one and when everyone had dried and put their pyjamas on the young ones would go straight to bed whilst the older ones would go downstairs for the usual jobs of darning and repairs to school clothes.

Meals also followed a routine, which never varied. Breakfast was prepared the night before. Miss Duncumb would prepare three slices of bread and dripping for each of us. These were then placed in a large bread bin ready for the following morning. There was no escape; everyone regardless of age and size had to eat their share. For some it was easy but others, particularly the younger ones, it was an ordeal having to eat so much but Miss Duncumb made no distinction between age and quantity. Dinner was a two-course meal and the menu for each day was always the same. After saying grace, we sat down to eat in silence. When she was in a good mood there would be a relaxed atmosphere and depending on what the dinner was, it was at times enjoyable. Friday was a day we dreaded more than any other. Without fail, fish was on the menu. Being close to the fishing port of Hull it was in plentiful supply and whoever was the errand boy at the time would collect the fish from the village fishmonger on Thursday after school. It was either Cod or Haddock. Each of us had a full-size fillet complete with skin and scales, boiled, not fried. It was served with very thin watery gravy poured over mashed potatoes. It was the most unappetizing meal of the week. Everything had to be eaten including the skin and scales. Once the fish course was over, we had our favourite pudding, jam roll, and custard.

A variety of puddings was served during the week including rice, tapioca, and semolina. For one of the boys, rice pudding was a nightmare. He had learning difficulties, which in those days was not recognized as it is today. He could not eat rice pudding and even worse for him was the skin. Miss Duncumb would stand behind him and clamping her huge hand over his chin would spoon feed him forcing the rice and skin into his mouth until he either swallowed it or choked. There was a similar incident experienced by one of the girls, but I did not see it myself. The girl who I have only the faintest memory of did write to me just a few years ago and which I still have the letter today. She had a problem eating food due to an intestinal problem brought about by Senna pod seeds lodged in her intestines. She had vomited during a meal and Miss Duncumb made her eat her own vomit. I was reluctant to include this incident as I had not seen it myself but whilst recently visiting Mrs. Sheena Staves, the daughter- in-law of Aunty Staves, she told me that her mother-in-law knew about the incident and had mentioned it to her. (See Appendix 3)

When she was in a bad mood, everyone kept very quiet and got on with the business of eating. Once dinner was over, we said Grace again and cleared the table. It was scrubbed whilst one of us did the washing up in the scullery. Twelve dinner plates, twelve pudding plates, cutlery for twelve, and pots and pan used in the cooking of the meal had to be washed and returned to the cupboard. The tea towels were washed and left to dry, and the draining board was scrubbed with a hard brush. At 4 o'clock the school bell would ring and for the 'home kids' it was a dash home for the usual clothing inspection, after which the cleaning and polishing would start all over again. A clothing inspection was carried out to see what had to be repaired or darned in readiness for the next day. In turn, each of us had to show the buttons on our jackets and trousers followed by our socks. We were split into two groups. The eldest six looked after the youngest six, any holes in the socks had to be darned, buttons missing sown back on and in addition, any repairs to the trousers was also done by the older boys. We had all been taught how to darn, patch and repair which although it was a chore we hated at the time, it was to prove invaluable in our later lives, especially for those of us who joined the Armed Forces for National Service, or for my brother Jim and myself who had signed on for longer careers.

Everyone had been given a job: boot cleaning, potato peeling, coal scuttle filling, cutlery cleaning, and laying the table for the evening tea. The younger children who did not have a job would sit in the dining room until tea was ready. During the times I handled the breakfast I would remove the bread from the bin and place six slices on six large plates placing them on the table between each pair. I then made the coffee (never tea) and poured one cup each for the twelve sitting at the table. On a Sunday whoever prepared the breakfast had to take Miss Dumcumb a cup of tea in bed, which was part of our duty. When the others had finished their work, they would come down for breakfast. For the Sunday breakfast, we had a boiled egg. I boiled the eggs counting to one hundred and twenty after the water had boiled. I rarely failed to get the timing to produce soft-boiled eggs which was much better than being hard-boiled. Miss Duncumb didn't seem to care that a twelve-year-old boy was handling a pan of boiling hot water over a gas flame unsupervised. She was always in bed on Sundays and just let us get on with our jobs and only appeared when we were getting ready to go to church.

Certain jobs had to be completed every day except Sunday. The back scullery where the potatoes and vegetables were kept had to be scrubbed each morning including the lavatory situated next to the coalhouse. The floor was concrete, about nine square yards in area. With a bucket of water, a hand scrubber, and a floor cloth, whoever had that job would kneel and scrub the floor after moving the sacks of vegetables out of the way. An area, depending on the length of reach by the one doing the cleaning had to be scrubbed and the next square had to overlap the preceding area so as not to leave a tidemark. In the scullery, someone else would be washing the breakfast plates, coffee cups, and other crockery before putting it away in a large cupboard in the kitchen. The scullery floor was scrubbed after we had washed and cleaned our teeth. Two washbasins served the twelve boys. A rack on the scullery wall with twelve hooks that held a towel, flannel, and a toothbrush, each one found by a number from one to twelve. My number was 8. Between the kitchen and the hallway was a lobby about ten feet long by three feet wide. There was a small cupboard with a single shelf and a larger cupboard above which was kept locked. The lower cupboard contained the second pair of boots for the twelve boys. Every morning the lower cupboard was emptied and scrubbed, even though it had not been used. To complete the job the floor was polished or scrubbed I cannot remember which. The second pair of boots were kept in the cupboard until required to replace those in use.

We were often late for school for several reasons. If Miss Duncumb was in a bad mood, she would make us sit at the table until everyone had eaten their breakfast. There was always one or two who could not eat very quickly, and the rest had to sit quietly waiting for them to finish so that we could leave the table. We changed into our school clothes and made a dash to school hoping to beat the starting bell. Anyone late had to wait outside the assembly hall until morning prayers were over. The latecomers were then called onto the front stage to explain to the headmaster Mr. Panky, who was not a very tolerant person, why we were late. Our explanation of having to work and then being kept at the table cut no ice with the Head. It was normally a few strokes of the cane on each hand but nothing as vicious as those we were used to at home. None of the teaching staff really believed our stories as it was accepted all the 'Home Kids' told lies or exaggerated their reasons for being late and the stories of our work every day.

Life would appear to be one long round of housework and punishment, but it did have its happier moments for two of us. Many of our school friends were from the wealthier families living in Cottingham. We would be invited to their birthday parties and sometimes to tea after school. Brian and Keith Williams often invited me to tea and on one occasion their parents took me to see the circus in Hull. Trevor Ashton was a great friend and I very rarely missed his parties. Ken Williamson, the son of potato merchant, never failed to invite me to his home for parties, and at times tea after school. Michael Jackson, the son of a fishing trawler owner was another of our friends and Roy Tiplady always let Albert Crooks and I ride his bike as well as invites to his home. Albert and I were the only two who seemed to get these invites and although Miss Duncumb didn't really like it, she couldn't stop us going as it would not have looked very good for her among those issuing the invitations. She did take us all to see the annual pantomime in Hull at the New Theater and every year we went to 'Hull Fair' one of the largest fairs in the country.

Being a member of the Boys Brigade gave me the opportunity to meet other boys from the Hull battalion when we attended annual camp and band practice in Hull most Saturday afternoons. These were happier times and it gave me an insight into what normal life should be. Those friends I made in the Boys Brigade are still friends today sixty-five years later and we remain in contact through the miracle of email and the web. The church of St Mary, the oldest and biggest church in the village, also played a great part in my early life. I did not like religion but all the children in the home were forced to attend the services regardless of their own preferences. We had to attend every service and event with the forty days of 'Lent' being the worst. Immediately after school the 'Home Kids' as we were known, would cross the road from the school straight into the church, which was only a minutes' walk away. Listening to something being said by an old vicar who did not share any goodwill towards the children from the home was always an ordeal we hated. Lent was followed by Easter and that, apart from Christmas, was my favourite event in the church calendar. Three of the boys from the home, myself included, had been recruited into the church choir. The organist and choirmaster was Mr. Wright a former POW who would never allow the Christmas Carol 'Silent Night' to be sung. He had heard it so many times by the Germans at a time when he and thousands of British soldiers were far away from home and locked in prison camps.

Being in the choir of twenty boys and twelve men, was a pleasure, except for the two nights we had to attend choir practice. On Sundays, those of us in the choir would dress in our cassock and surplice and do a grand entry into the choir stalls after having slowly walked up the side aisle on the right of the church and then down the center aisle into the choir stalls singing my favourite hymns. Three girls sat in the front pew just across from the choir stalls making eyes at the two head boys. Carolyn Fussy, Diane Polly, and Pam Dow, three ladies of prominent families of the village. After I left the homes I kept in touch with Pam, Carolyn, and Trevor Ashton. Sadly, Pam died a few years later but I remain good friends with Carolyn and Trevor.

The highlight of the year for the choirboys was Carol Singing. For three nights, we would visit many houses around Cottingham by invitation and sing carols by request. Without fail, the very appreciative people made a good donation. Christmas Eve was reserved for the pubs. We would stand in the foyer and sing our hearts out and the usual cacophony of sound would reduce as the choir of twenty choristers sang all the most popular carols. Frank and Trevor would go around the revellers with the collection boxes swelling the contents of the already heavy tins. The two head boys would share out the proceeds, no doubt on a sliding scale as to each boy's position in the choir. We still had to attend church on Christmas day. for Holy Communion at 8am followed 'Matins' at 11am.

The only Christmas tree was in Miss Duncumb's sitting room, but we did help to put up the decorations. Dinner was always accompanied by visits from the local councillor and the church vicar. Mr. Arbon and the Reverend Hebron would give the twelve of us sitting at the table a sixpence each. These, with the one we would find in our Christmas pudding, put there by Miss Duncumb would go into our savings. We were also given fourpence a month pocket money but not allowed to spend it until some special occasion came up, or we could go to the local Saturday afternoon cinema. Miss Duncumb did try to make Christmas day special and Christmas dinner was always of the highest quality considering the food rationing at the time. I can only remember receiving two presents. The first one was a wooden model of a tank made by a wounded soldier in rehabilitation. The following year it was a kaleidoscope, a three-sided mirror tube with coloured beads, which could be shaken to form the beads in hundreds of different patterns.

Shortly after the war had ended and during Christmas, the twelve of us each received a letter and card from a family in America. The card I received was from a family who owned a turkey farm. I replied to the letter but that was the end of any communication. Christmas should be a happy occasion but even though we were well fed and sitting with a fire giving off a pleasant warmth the thing missing for me was my mam my brothers, and my sisters.

In 1948 it was decided that the children in the homes of Yorkshire should have a holiday in one of the coastal towns of the county. Withernsea being selected in preference to Bridlington, Filey, and Hornsea, all far superior to Withernsea, but magic to the Gray family as that is where our mother was still living and there was every possibility, we would be able to see her. On the day of our departure, a single deck coach arrived to pick us up and take us to Withernsea. We were accommodated in the classrooms of Withernsea High School sleeping on mattresses laid on the floor. Being a school, it had ample kitchen facilities to comfortably provide three meals a day for over a hundred excited and energetic young children. The sports field was huge, and it was not long before football and cricket games were being played. The first meal was at about 5 o'clock. The other holidaymakers from Bridlington and Driffield were sitting at their tables when the Cottingham kids made their appearance.

The noise was tremendous with all the others laughing and shouting as they waited for their food to be served. We marched into the dining hall in pairs, straight to our table not uttering a sound. As we passed one of the tables to our left, I saw Jack, Jim, and Freda. I shouted out to try to attract their attention, but Miss Duncumb said, 'Fred Gray be quiet'. We sat down at our allotted table and after saying Grace we ate our meal in silence. As soon as the meal was over, and Grace had been said we dashed out onto the playing fields where I was reunited with my two brothers and sister Freda for the first time since June 1944. I did not even know which home they were in or where it was.

The following day was even more momentous for the four of us. Sometime during the day when we were out on the playing field, someone came over to us and said, 'your mam is over in the corner of the field.' We looked over and sure enough, our mam was sitting on the grass in the far corner. We raced over and we were all over her giving her hugs and trying to kiss her. There were a lot of tears that day and for the first time in over four years, five of our family was together again. What a wonderful time we had, and mam came to see us every day until the holiday was over.

One year after the Withernsea holiday the authorities decided that those children separated during the war years should be reunited. Brothers and sisters were to live together. Jim Jack and Freda came to live with me in Cottingham and it was not to be a happy reunion for them. Whilst in the Driffield home they lived a life of relative freedom and happiness with a very pleasant matron. Freda was too young to really understand what was happening and Jack and Jim took an instant dislike to the Cottingham home. Miss Duncumb also took an instant dislike to Jack, and Jim was not happy about the situation either. Jack at once fell afoul of Miss Duncumb with his outspoken remarks and telling her he wanted to go back to Driffield. A few raps of the cane soon persuaded him it was best to accept the situation and keep his remarks to himself. The three of them soon fell into the routine of the house but never came to accept the conditions under which they now lived. Both Jim and Jack did run away on two occasions but were soon caught and returned to Cottingham. They slept in the same room as me whilst Freda shared the back bedroom with three other girls whom she had never met before.

For Freda, breakfast and the three slices of bread and dripping became an ordeal. She had to eat just the same amount as the older boys and although I sat opposite her, I could not help her out as Miss Duncumb stood at the end of the table with arms folded across her chest watching like a hawk to make sure no one helped her. Because it took so long for Freda to eat her breakfast it would often mean the rest of us could not leave the table and get ready for school, resulting in us being late many times. When the girls came to live with us the discipline did ease slightly. Instead of the cane, the girls would have so many slaps with a female type hairbrush. Still painful but nothing compared to the cane which was still used on the boys. Other things also changed. We could keep outdoor pets such as rabbits and pigeons. My friends the Wilson brothers gave me several pigeons and they helped me to build a loft for them. Two rabbits were donated by a rabbit breeder to Thomas Charlton and two more for the remainder of us. I longed for a bike and I was able to take a job as an errand boy with the local grocer Mr. Mudd. I was paid five shillings a week plus tips. The delivery transport was a bicycle with a large cage on the front for carrying the boxes of groceries. Mrs. Staves lent me the money to buy a bicycle (£5) and I could pay her back on a weekly basis. Everything went well for a few weeks and then disaster struck. One of the boys who had been released from the home previously decided he would pay us a visit and bring a present. John Smith lived on a farm in Holm-on-Spalding Moor, about fifteen miles from Cottingham. Being on a farm he had access to air guns and air pistols and thought a pistol would make a nice present!

He gave me the pistol and I had to hide it in my pigeon loft. Sometime later one of the pigeons laid an egg. Being so pleased with it I told the other boys and one of them told Miss Duncumb. She went down the garden to look at our latest arrival and that's when the thunder struck. She found the air pistol. Apart from the cane, I lost my job as an errand boy and I had to get rid of the pigeons. Thomas Charlton who had nothing to do with the gun also suffered. His rabbits, which he gave so much care and attention as they were the first things he had ever had in his life that he could call his own. Thomas was a true orphan and had never known his parents and was heartbroken when he had to return them to the original owner. Miss Duncumb said he had neglected the animals and was no longer able to look after them. That left us with two other rabbits, one of them a 'Blue Angora' a most beautiful animal.

As I was the dog walker, I used to collect rabbit food on my long walks with Gyp. The problem arose when someone else took my job and I was not allowed to collect any rabbit food. This was part of my punishment for the gun affair. Worse still, Miss Duncumb would not allow me to give the rabbits any food from the vegetable sack in the back scullery. I was not allowed to go anywhere near the hutch and the rabbits were to suffer because of it. When the winter started, they were getting less and less food and eventually they died, the Blue Angora first and the second one a few days later. I buried them both in the garden and I believe to this day Miss Duncumb deliberately starved those rabbits to punish me. After I lost my job as an errand boy, I could not pay Mrs. Staves her money back. I asked her to speak to Miss Duncumb and explain to her about the loan. I assume she didn't want Mrs. Staves to suffer for my actions, so I could ask Mr. Mudd for my job back. Once the loan had been paid off, I lost my job again, but I still had the bike. As I was due to leave the home in a few weeks' time she may have realized I needed a bike if I was to find work in Hull.

The day I had been longing for came sometime in July 1950. It was before the school holidays started as all the others had left for school, but I was told to stay behind. I had no idea why! I was given a small suitcase and was told to pack my belongings as I was leaving for Hull. When I was ready, I walked round to the front of the house with my bike and with Miss Duncumb carrying my case, we walked to the railway station only a short distance away. When the train arrived, I put my bike into the guard's van and took a seat in one of the carriages. She didn't say anything to me except to tell me someone would meet me at Hull Paragon Station, and with that, I was a free fifteen-year-old boy not knowing where I was to live or how I was to earn a living. The man who was waiting for me was a total stranger and I did not even know his name, but he seemed to know me. He was the person who would handle my welfare and to help me find a job.

To the very end of my six years and two months in that ugly house with a monstrous woman who should never have been allowed to look after children, I hated about every minute I lived there. Mrs. Staves was our relief valve and on Tuesday and Thursday when she came to look after us there was always sunshine over the house regardless of the time of year. The atmosphere in the house changed when she was there but the dark clouds soon came back when Miss Duncumb returned from her day spent in Beverley with her aging mother. Mrs Staves was a lovely lady, loved by us all. From about 1948 every Tuesday and Thursday evening I would escort Mrs. Staves back to her home near the Cottingham recreation ground after Miss Duncumb had returned from her day off. Due to the lateness of the hour, I stayed overnight, sleeping in Malcolm's room (Mrs Staves son) It was here I was to experience what a real home should be like. When I came downstairs in the morning, the fire was already alight and throwing out a nice warm heat in a very pleasant room. I sat at the table and Aunty Staves would serve me with a breakfast after which I had to leave and dash back to my real existence. I didn't even have to say Grace! Malcolm was a serving officer in the Royal Air Force flying in Lancaster bombers over Germany and survived the war. Malcolm and I became good friends and I still visited him at his home in Cottingham until he tragically died in 2014.

Mrs. Sheena Staves, Miss Duncumb, 'Aunty' Staves

Part Two

Chapter 5

Starting a new life

I was fifteen years old when I left the home in 1950. I had no certificates of education, no job, and no income. I left Miss Duncumb on Cottingham railway station platform without either of us saying anything other than her telling me I would be met at Hull Paragon station by a person unknown to me and he would take me to my new home, wherever that was, and with that, she went out of my life. The man who was waiting for me was a total stranger and I did not even know his name, but he knew me. It turned out he was the person who would be responsible for my welfare and to help me find a job. We walked to Linnaeus Street on Hessle Road, about a mile from the station. We arrived at a large house and entered through the front door into a spacious hallway. The person who greeted us was dressed in a uniform and I was to find out later the 'Church Army' administered this 'Youth Hostel'.

The other occupants of the hostel were a mixture of working-class boys and nautical sea cadet students attending Hull Nautical College. There were fifty cadets accommodated on the second floor of the house and fifteen working-class lads on the third floor (the attic). Although I was working-class, I shared a room with a police cadet on the second floor. He was not a very pleasant character and did not like sharing a room with anyone else and became very abusive when two more cadets arrived and moved into the same room. They were older than me and would not put up with his attitude and told him so. Being two big Yorkshire lads, the police cadet soon realized he could not intimidate them, but it left an awfully bad atmosphere in the room. All the facilities, i.e. the dining room, TV room, table tennis room, and the snooker table were shared between the two groups but fights often broke out between the working-class lads and the cadets who thought they were far superior to the other lads and did not hesitate to make their difference in class known. The first meal we had was tea at about 5pm. All the meals were served through a small hatch between the kitchen and dining room. At the end of the meal, the crockery and cutlery were returned through the same hatch.

The day after my arrival at the hostel the same person who had brought me there took me to locations in Hull where I might like to work. Our first port of call was at a boat marina where I was given the offer of becoming a 'rigger', which I immediately turned down. I told him I wanted to be a joiner and work with wood. We left the marina for the next location and drove down Anlaby Road to Nornabell Street in east Hull. When he pulled up at our next location, we were opposite a small archway that had a title board above the arch which displayed the company name 'Beard and Butlins. Joiners and Undertakers'. In the next few months, I was to learn far more about undertaking than joinery. There was one other joiner working there but soon after I had started work, he left for another job, leaving me the only employee. I did go out on one job with him just before he left. It was cleaning the gutters of the Nautical College in Hull. The ladder that we had to reach the roof was not long enough and fell about two feet short underneath the roof edge. He went up the ladder first and when he got as far as he could go, he reached up and hauled himself up over the parapet onto the roof. I followed as far as I could, then reached up to catch hold of his hand, so that he could haul me up over the roof edge. When the job was complete it was in reverse. He lowered me down until I reached the top rung of the ladder and very carefully felt my way lower until I was able to feel the second or third rung and then continue to ground level. It was, to say the least, a very dangerous situation as I could have fallen had I not been able to hold onto his outstretched hand. (no health and safety in those days)!!

During the first week, I also accompanied the boss to a house where an old lady had died, and we were there to pick up her body and take it back to our yard where there was a small Chapel of Rest. After the dead person had been prepared and dressed for burial by my boss, it stayed there until the funeral directors took it away for burial or cremation. It was the first time I had seen a dead person and the boss gave me the head end to get the lady from her bed into an outsize coffin, which was used for collecting the dead from homes if that is where they had died. The coffin was left over from the war years and had been used to collect air raid victims, often after being blown to pieces. There were still bits of evidence that the 'Shell' as it was called, had not been cleaned properly when the war had finished.

The coffins were made from 'flat packs' which I had to collect from a local supplier. I loaded three or four packs onto a hand cart and started my journey back to the yard. The cart had two large iron clad wheels. and a handle about four feet long with a short handle fixed across the end to hold onto. I pushed the load through the heavy traffic, of one of the main artery roads of Hull. At that time of the day, there were hundreds of workers on bicycles, in cars, or in electrically driven trolley buses all trying to get to work. Close to the yard one of the wheels of the cart hit an obstruction or a pothole in the road surface. I didn't have any means of securing the packs and they slid down off the cart onto the road, leaving me with a neat pile of flat pack coffins, with cyclists, cars, and trolley buses, all trying to get past me. I loaded the packs back onto the cart by myself, as not one single person stopped to give me any help. When I did finally reload them, I finished my journey back to the yard in Nornabell Street which was less the ten minutes away.

The first floor of the workshop was full of old ready assembled coffins leaning against the wall and with very dim lighting, it made a frightening place for a fifteen-year-old. That was where I had to sit to eat my sandwiches at lunchtime, surrounded by coffins and there were no facilities to wash my hands. After a few months, I had had enough of this job and left without giving notice. I can't remember how much I was paid but it was very poor, no more than £2 per week. I didn't have to pay for my lodging in the hostel, so my pay was just enough to see me through the week.

I soon found another job working in a sawmill. One of the other working-class lads introduced me to the foreman and I was taken on as a 'backer'. All I had to do was stand behind one of the huge circular saws and stack the timber on a pallet as the 'sawyer' cut the timber to a specific required size. When the pallet had the required amount on it, I would use a trolley jack to take it to the loading bay, where it was put onto a large flat-bed trailer ready for distribution around the country. It was a job that required no experience and there was nothing that would be of any use for other employment, but it was easy, and I got on very well with the workforce. Two or three weeks after starting work at the timber yard the same person who had met me at the station arrived and told me I was to be an apprentice cabinetmaker with the largest furniture manufacturer in Hull. I was taken to a tool company and given all the tools I would need for my apprenticeship. This was the start of five years of boredom and little learning of how to make furniture. I did quite a lot of joinery as the company also employed joiners for outside work fitting out pubs, cargo ships, factories and various other places around the city. I preferred this side of the job to staying in the workshop standing at a workbench all day being controlled by a buzzer, which would signal the start and end of each day including the ten-minute break in the morning and afternoon.

In the winter months, the workshop was freezing cold in the morning and only began to heat up two or three hours after the large boiler in the basement had been lit and produced enough heat to make comfortable working conditions. It took well over an hour to have any effect in the workshop, but this was the conditions people worked under a few years after the war had ended.

My new employers were the Armstrong's, a family of four, a father and three sons. None of them were over five feet tall but they had the workforce of cabinetmakers, joiners, and machinists, apprehensive with the possibility of losing their jobs when orders for the furniture slowed down. Every Friday afternoon at 3 o'clock the eldest of the brothers would strut down the centre aisle of the workshop showing to the manager which of the craftsmen were to be laid off at two hours' notice. There was never any interaction between owners and employees. It was as though the Armstrong family held their workforce in total contempt. They would never smile or acknowledge any of those skilled men, most of whom had fought in the war, including one, a former paratrooper who had lost his leg during the Battle of Arnhem. I was never happy for the whole of my five years working for the Armstrong's and couldn't wait for it to end so that I could do what I really wanted to and join the British Army.

After living in the hostel for about six months I made my first friends when I joined the 24th Hull Company of the Boys Brigade at the age of sixteen and met up with some of the lads I knew from our annual camps at various locations around Yorkshire during my years in the home. I became very friendly with all the seniors and I have maintained contact with at least fifteen of them who now live in England, Canada, Australia, and New Zealand. The friendship is still strong and holds to the present time. I also met Malcolm Tilling for the first time who was a member of the youth club on Newland Avenue Hull, which most of the lads from the Boy's Brigade were members. Later he asked me if I would like to live with his family instead of the hostel. Without hesitation, I said yes and went to see Malcolm's parents living in Park Avenue, and there I met Mr and Mrs Tilling their daughter Janet and younger brother Michael who agreed I was to live with the family. It was a 'Foster' arrangement with the Beverley Council paying Mrs Tilling an amount of money on a weekly basis for my lodgings. I stayed with the family until I joined the Army in 1956. They considered me a member of their family and I have kept in contact with them to the present day.

My National Service commitment had been deferred until I was twenty-one so at the age of nineteen, I joined 299 Parachute Squadron Royal Engineers based in Hull. It was here I met some of the finest men anyone could wish to know. They were all paratroopers, and many had seen action in some of the fiercest battles of the war including Arnhem and the River Rhine crossing in March 1945. I was sent on a parachute jumping course and completed two jumps from a captive balloon cage and a further six from a military aircraft which gave me the right to wear a parachute wings arm badge and the coveted 'Red Beret 'The unit was a Territorial Army Parachute Squadron, part of the 44th Parachute Brigade (TA).

I could now look forward to joining the regular army when I was twenty-one. Unfortunately, I broke my leg on my thirteenth parachute jump which delayed my entry into the army by a year, When I was eventually called up for my National Service, I was already a trained parachutist and a semi-trained soldier, but the deferment was to cost me dear, later in my career.

I was called up for National Service in 1956. Because of my experience with the Territorial Army, I was immediately selected for the Royal Engineers and after basic training, and two brutal selection courses for Airborne Forces, I completed a second parachute course and was posted to 9 Parachute Squadron Royal Engineers based in Aldershot, Hampshire. I was soon to learn life in a parachute squadron was different from any other regiments and squadrons in the Corps of Royal Engineers. A much higher standard of fitness, and readiness to move to any part of the world at short notice was a requisite. A very famous high-ranking officer said of the Squadron 'Arguably the best minor unit in the British Army. I had joined the elite!

In September 1959 after a five months tour in Cyprus and Jordan, I had the good fortune to meet Betty Anne Whitman, the girl who was to become my wife. Not only did I meet my future wife, but I also gained a brother-in-law. A wonderful character who has made me laugh more than any other person I know. We have never had a cross word in the fifty-nine years I have known him. If ever a wife was made to be an Army wife, it was Betty. She immediately took to the rigours of constantly moving to other parts of the world at short notice, never complaining and never owning the contents of the quarters we lived in. Long separations at short notice is an accepted way of life in a parachute unit and Betty never failed to meet the problems encountered by service wives when their husbands had been called away. She also became extremely popular with other wives of the unit and 'the lads' because of her ready smile and friendship.

Reluctantly I had to leave the parachute squadron in July 1961, shortly after the birth of our son James David, for a posting to Malaya. It was a posting necessary to help with further promotion prospects as the parachute squadron was a closed shop as far as promotions above the rank of Staff Sergeant was concerned.

Malaya was a three-year tour, which was an incredible experience. Almost non-stop sunshine, a servant paid for by the government, superb living quarters, and a very good social life for the families. A few days after our arrival in Penang I met Malcolm Tilling and his wife Anne. He was serving with the RAF and they lived just a few hundred yards from our quarters. I had no idea he was living there until I saw him on the bus, which took RAF and Army soldiers to the ferry terminal each morning for the crossing from Penang to Butterworth on the mainland where our units were stationed. It was good to see friends again who had been in location for a few months and knew the ropes. For the soldiers, it was constant training in Jungle warfare with other units of the 28th Commonwealth Brigade: a force of about four and a half thousand men made up of British, Australians, and New Zealanders.

Tours to other countries did cause a great deal of separation for the families but friends and wives clubs and many activities, i.e. beach clubs, sailing, shooting clubs, basketball tournaments and visits to Singapore helped to keep the families occupied during the long separations. My squadron; 11 Independent Field Squadron RE, made tours to North Borneo (4 months), Thailand (3months), Sarawak (3 Months) and many other short tours in Singapore and Blakang Mati, a small island off the coast of Singapore used as a POW camp for British and Australian soldiers during the 2nd World War.. The Far East tour ended in 1964 and I returned to 9 Parachute Squadron with the rank of Sergeant, and it wasn't too long before the squadron was off again. This time to Kenya for three months, Aden for three months and Libya for six weeks.

During this period of my career, I was promoted to Staff Sergeant, but this rank was the highest available in the squadron except for Sergeant Major, for which the vacancy only occurred every two years. I did a four months Quartermasters Sergeant Instructors Course (QMSI) at the Royal Engineers School of Military Engineering Chatham that qualified me for the rank of Warrant Officer Class 2. To further my prospects, I was posted to Germany to join 1st Field Squadron Royal Engineers based in Nienburg. After a superb two-year tour, I was selected for an instructor's post with the Royal Canadian Engineers at Chilliwack in British Columbia Canada.

We had two wonderful years in Canada, and we lived in the most beautiful part of British Columbia. We joined the ski club on the base and during the long winter months skied most weekends. We all became reasonable skiers, but our son Jim became a real expert and during his army career skied for his regiment, the Grenadier Guards, and later he qualified as a BASI (British Association of Ski Instructors). Living in British Columbia we took the opportunity to visit the West Coast of the USA taking in the Redwoods of Oregon, San Francisco, Los Angeles, Hollywood, San Diego, and Tijuana in Mexico, returning north via Hoover Dam, Lake Mead, Las Vegas, and Yellowstone Park. Sadly, in 1974 we had to return to Europe and BAOR (British Army of the Rhine) at the end of a memorable tour with the Canadian Engineers.

I took up the post of Squadron Sergeant Major of 42 Field Squadron based in Hameln (home of the fabled 'Pied piper) in West Germany. I had a bad start to the appointment with the Officer Commanding the Squadron. He did not like me, and I did not like him. Fortunately, he departed for civilian life four months later and one of the best officers I met during my service took over command of the Squadron. From then on it was a pleasant two -year tour in one of the ancient towns of Germany. At the end of my tour as SSM, I returned to Canada to the British Army Training Unit Suffield (BATUS) in Alberta as QMSI in charge of the live firing ranges, which were used for training the armoured and infantry regiments of the British Army in tactics using live ammunition. Six months late r I returned to BAOR and after a four-month course in 'Work-Study' at Shrivenham. I was posted to Willich, a major stores depot on the Dutch/German border. My experience here was one of boredom and frustration with the inactivity and having to work with one of the army's worst officers I had the misfortune to meet. I had been promoted to Warrant Officer Class 1 but not as a Regimental Sergeant Major, which had been my ambition from the day I first joined the army twenty-two years previously.

To be selected as an RSM I had to be thirty-eight at the time of promotion. I was one year past the age required basically because I did not join the army until I was twenty-two which had put me well behind those who joined at the age of eighteen or who had been 'Boy Soldiers'. Breaking my leg had delayed me joining the army by one year and was also a factor in my being over the age limit. I did not consider a commission and I left the army after twenty-three years, disappointed because I did not make Regimental Sergeant Major, which was my ambition from the first day, I joined the British Army in 1956.

I took a temporary job in a warehouse whilst I was waiting for the result of an interview for employment with the Ministry of Defense as a Military Courier. I was fortunate enough to be selected out of three hundred applicants, and it was the start of an amazing period in my life. I started work in February 1980. This was the start of twenty-one years of non-stop travel, by road and by air. Although officially I was a civil servant, I was employed by the Ministry of Defense to take highly classified material to all parts of the UK and worldwide. In twenty-one years, I travelled nine and a half million miles by air and many thousands by road. The countries I visited ranged from Iceland in the north to New Zealand in the south and Hawaii in the west to Hong Kong in the east and many more in between. I retired from the Civil Service in 2000 and Betty and I immediately booked a three months world tour taking in Thailand, Singapore Malaysia, Australia, and New Zealand, and a second tour two years later.

In 1985, a group of former 9 Squadron friends formed the 'Airborne Engineers Association.' Of which I was a founder member. The association rapidly grew to over a thousand members. During the various functions and reunions, I was to meet up with many of those I served with during my twelve years with 9 Parachute Squadron, many of them living in the county of Hampshire. Betty and I celebrated our Golden Wedding anniversary in 2010 with our son Jim and our three wonderful grandsons: Peter, Michael, and Robert. We also had eighty other members of our extended family and friends and neighbours at the party, organized by Jim and our daughter-in-law Carole. After several moves, we finally settled in Fleet Hampshire thirty years ago. Our son Jim with his wife Carole and son's live in Sandhurst, Berkshire about a fifteen-minute drive from Fleet.

Back Row: Michael, Robert, Peter
Jim and Carole

Chapter 6

June Elizabeth Hare (Lockwood)

1928-2007

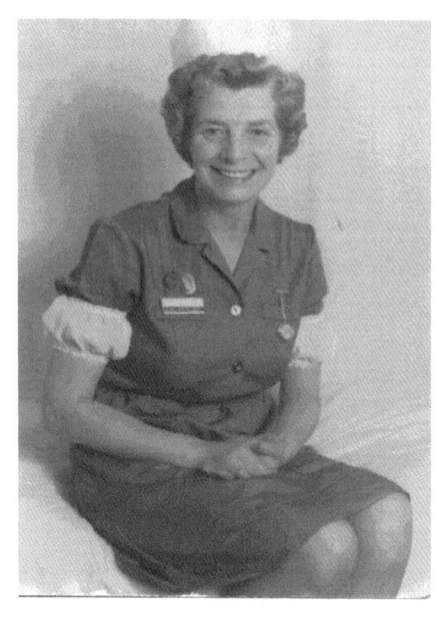

Although June was born a Lockwood in reality, she was a Gray. She was always our 'big sister' and she bore the responsibility of looking after her younger brothers and sisters. She attended the local school close to where we lived but as with most of the children of her generation schooling was basic and not a preparation for future years. She was able to play a few tunes on the school piano but that was a natural talent and not one acquired by piano lessons. Her education was interrupted by the outbreak of the 2nd World War and she left school at the age of fourteen. As she grew older, she developed a more sophisticated liking for music, art, and much later in her life, the beauty of the Yorkshire Dales but her early life had been a struggle, as it was for most people in our class of society. She met her future husband, William (Bill) Hare and they were married on 24 April 1947, June was eighteen years old. They had to live with her husband's parents, and they had three children, Christine, Doreen, and David. Living with her in-laws in a small house was not an ideal way to start a family and her life was one long struggle to bring up her three children.

There were no modern amenities in the house and the washing of clothing was done in the old fashioned 'Dolly Tub' and then hung out on the line to dry. Most of the housekeeping also fell to June as her in-laws were quite elderly and left most of the chores to her. It truly was a drudge of an existence. Her difficulties increased when Jim and I came home on leave and stayed with her and the family. She never complained and always made us most welcome even though her husband was on a poor wage and our presence did not help matters. Bill was a very gentle type of person and very set in his ways. He loved snooker and became very skillful. He never missed his one night a week visit to his club and was never seen without a cigarette between his lips.

During his wartime service, he suffered from what was known as 'shell-shock', a mental condition that was to stay with him for the rest of his life. Today the same condition is known as 'Post Traumatic Stress Disorder' and is treatable, but the only treatment he received was being strapped to a bed and given a series of electric shocks which was more like torture than a cure. He was a chain smoker, and it was almost inevitable, he would develop cancer, which he did, and sadly he died on the 30th October 1981.

When her three children became self-sufficient and married, June was able to turn her attention to the things she had wanted to do earlier in life. She took a three-year nursing course and qualified as a State Enrolled Nurse. With further study, she qualified as a State Registered Nurse but after twenty-seven years of nursing at the Hull Royal Infirmary, she retired. The constant lifting of heavy patients had taken its toll on her own health and she could no longer bend or walk without pain. After her retirement, she became a reading assistant at a local school where she helped children with reading disabilities. She became very friendly with Mrs. Jean Moore and her sister Eileen and they enjoyed travelling together to all parts of England and venturing abroad to the Continent. They had formed a lunch club with Jean's sister and two other friends.

The friendship between June and Jean lasted for over forty years. June also developed an interest in cricket, especially the Yorkshire County Cricket Club, often travelling to matches at the county ground to watch her special team. She started a collection of quality 'limited editions' of famous horses including 'Burmese' the gift of the Royal Canadian Mounted Police to her H.M. the Queen that she rode to her birthday parade for many years. She had a love of classical music, especially the 'Tenors.' In 2007 knowing that she was dying she asked that a recording of 'Nessun Dorma 'sung by her beloved tenor, Pavarotti, be played at her funeral. Her legacy was thirty grand and great-grandchildren, most of who were at her farewell. A much-loved sister, mother, grandmother, and friend of many

June with her grand- daughters and great grand children

George William Gray
1930-2012

My eldest brother George was a complex character with a volatile temperament. He had a fearful temper and at times he would strike out at anyone who annoyed him. From an early age, George suffered from poor eyesight, probably caused by some childhood disease. He started Infant's school at the age of five until it was interrupted by the start of the Second World War in 1939. During his evacuation to Lincolnshire, there was no education and when he rejoined his family in Withernsea his attendance at school was very spasmodic and he stayed away most of the time, refusing to attend mainly because of the teacher's inability to see that he had difficulty in seeing the blackboard because of his poor eyesight. He, along with Fred, Jack, Jim and Freda were taken into care and it was the only settled period of schooling he had but that ended five months later when he reached the age of fifteen. He left school without any certificates of achievement.

His first employment was on a farm near to the Patrington workhouse. He could read but found writing difficult. He stayed in farming for a few years moving from farm to farm in the East Riding of Yorkshire. The pay was poor, but he loved the outdoor life. He had no love for horses and was indifferent to the farm dogs but enjoyed milking the cows, singing as he milked them in the old traditional way.

Not all the farms he worked on were enjoyable. In one incident, he saved the farmer from severe injury when a bull attacked him. George drove the animal away with a pitchfork but was gored in his lower side just above the hipbone. The farmer saw no need to thank George for his act of bravery but carried on as though it was a normal happening on a farm. Working seven days a week for no extra pay and conditions on the farm going from bad to worse he decided to leave and find work elsewhere. When the farmer's wife heard he was leaving; she tried to stop him by blocking the farm gate and threatening him with a shotgun. He called her bluff and walked away carrying all his possessions in one small suitcase.

He soon found other work but this time erecting large barns, which required a certain amount of skill and was easily within George's scope. He had teamed up with our brother Jack who had recently left the Army after his two-year stint as a National Serviceman. Together they turned to bigger and higher steel construction in the towns and cities of Yorkshire. They got on very well together and enjoyed the single life of young men. There was no shortage of female company and the social pub life of Withernsea provided all the entertainment they could ask for. After a few years working together, Jack went his own way and set up a small business in Hull repairing and selling vacuum cleaners. George also moved on to other employment including maintenance on the television masts around northern England. He had no fear of heights and often worked, sometimes in freezing weather, at heights of eight hundred feet without safety harnesses or hard helmets.

With the arduous work and outdoor life George had become much stronger and stood six feet tall. He looked after his physical health, but his eyesight was causing him a lot of concern. He was never without lady friends, some of whom became his partner and set up house in Withernsea. Unfortunately, because he would not give a long-term commitment, they left him, some after a few months and others much longer.

Finally, he did meet and marry Joyce Horner and together they brought up three sons: Derek, Michael, and Robert. When they reached maturity, they all stand over six feet tall and are three sons any parents would be proud of. Before moving to Withernsea, George and Joyce rented a house in Woodall Street in the city of Hull where they raised their sons. The marriage was not to last and after eleven years they divorced. Joyce remarried but tragically she died from heart failure whilst on holiday in Italy leaving George with the responsibility of seeing his sons through the most important years of their lives, a responsibility he was not equipped for.

George continued with his nomadic life in the steel erecting business riding his powerful Arial Square-four 1000cc motorcycle, mostly without proper clothing, gloves, or a helmet. Inevitably, he did have an accident when he was involved with a truck, but not seriously hurt. The motorbike ended up in a ditch and he left it there never going back for it. That was the end of his motorcycling days.

A change of employment from steel erecting to the local Gas Board gave him a more settled life. He was living in Withernsea with various partners but once again he would not commit to any prolonged period with the same person. He commuted between Hull and Withernsea with his workmates at the gas board and for the next few years was employed on emergency call outs for gas leaks in the distribution system. Living in Withernsea suited him as he had many friends and mates in the town and joined with them in a bodybuilding club and enjoying the social life of the clubs and pubs and lots of ladies, one of whom moved in with him. She was an attractive lady but wanted more than just looking after a man with problems who refused to make a long-term commitment to her. Finally, she left to start a new life of her own. At the end of his working life, George retired from the Gas Board with a small pension and a gratuity for the years he had worked with the company. He met a divorced lady and they set up home at No 1 Hull Road Withernsea.

This was the start of his downward spiral to alcoholism and mental deterioration. He loved to see his grandchildren but was beyond being able to care for them. He was smoking cigarettes almost continuously and drinking beer from cans at home as well as enjoying the pub life with his partner. It was not long before his gratuity was used up and with failing eyesight and his mental state deteriorating the inevitable happened and his partner left him, although they stayed good friends for the remainder of his life.

His eyesight and the mental condition worsened, and Derek, Robert, and Michael became concerned for his safety around the house with the possibility of him falling over and hurting himself. Derek lived in Italy with his wife and family and was unable to offer much in the way of help being so far away. Michael gave assistance whenever he could, but it fell to Robert to become the main carer. He gave up his well-paid job in the steel erecting business so he could stay at home and be a full- time career to his dad. He took up employment at the local school as a caretaker, which gave him the opportunity to call in to check on George to make sure he was coping and looking after himself. On occasions, George would leave the house and wander off not knowing where he was going or where he had been. It became even more dangerous when he left his home and wandered onto country roads at night. Robert resorted to locking the doors after dark so that his dad could not wander off again.

Inevitably, George had to be taken into care and was placed in a home in Withernsea only a mile from his home. Robert and Michael visited often but after a few months his mental health broke down completely. He had no recognition of visitors other than Robert who had borne the burden of care for such a long time. George passed away in 2012 and was buried in the cemetery at the top of 'England's Hill' just over a mile outside of Withernsea. His grave is only a few yards away from our mother's small monument in the same cemetery. His funeral service was well attended by family and friends and many of the older generations of Withernsea people would remember him as one of the most colorful characters.

Sally
1933-1983

After the death of her wealthy employer Sally, as she was now known, took up employment in the Kodak film laboratory in Ilford. She had a regular boyfriend who we only knew as Alan. They had been together for a good few years and Sally had made more contact with her family, especially June, and often came back to Hull to stay with her for short holidays. She also made a visit to Betty and me in Germany where we took her to the Hartz Mountains to see the 'Wall', which separated East Germany from the West. She also came to Farnborough in Hampshire and was able to watch the Queen's Birthday Parade on Horse Guards London. It was during this visit that it became apparent she was suffering from some serious medical problems. It was cancer. She made no fuss and insisted on doing everything herself without inconveniencing others. She had become awfully close to George and they would sit for hours talking about religion and how it could solve all the World's problems, instead of it causing them. Nothing could change their minds and they were both very right-wing in their politics. It seemed to give them both comfort and they were convinced it was the answer to all their own personal problems.

Despite chemotherapy treatment, her cancer became more serious and at the early age of fifty she died in hospital in Brentwood. June and my wife Betty were at her bedside when she died. The police had informed my employers that she was in the hospital and had very little time left. I was on Courier Duty and a relief courier was sent up to Blackpool to the hotel where I was staying to take over my consignment. I made the mad dash back to Brentwood to be with her, but I was too late. By the time I reached the hospital, she had passed away no more than an hour earlier. Her employers at the film laboratory had given Sally a very generous sum of £10,000 for her enforced early retirement. In her will, she donated £5000 to the 'Donkey Sanctuary' and £5000 to the 'Cats Home' which would take care of her five cats for the remainder of their lives. That at least would have given Sally peace of mind knowing she had contributed to something she cared so passionately about.

John David (Jack)
1937-1971

John David was born in 1937 in Paradise Place on the same birth date as our mother 26th May. He was the third of four sons and christened John David but always known to the family as Jack.. I have little memory of him during his early years or whilst we were in the workhouse. He was evacuated in September 1939 with June and me to the village of Fishwort near Boston in Lincolnshire. I do remember him crying a great deal when he was outside the house with June sitting in a small field or paddock where we were living. I was inside with Mr. Grant, a farmer, who had taken a liking to me, possibly because he had no son of his own, only a daughter. June told me years later, because of Jack's constant fretting we had to return to Hull, as the family could not cope with his constant disruption to their family life.

From June 1944 to 1950 he was in a children's home, with Jim and Freda in the small market town of Driffield in Yorkshire. By the standards of the Cottingham children's home, they lived in a happy house with lots of freedom and excellent care from the matron. Sometime in 1950, it was decided that families should be brought back together resulting in my three siblings being transferred to Cottingham.

It was not a happy move for them. Jack found the discipline very hard and was often in trouble with Miss Duncumb. At an early stage of his development, he was becoming quite rebellious which created problems for him later in life. After being discharged from the home in 1952 he joined the army as a 'Boy Entrant'. Very soon he took his first steps on the promotion ladder, eventually reaching the rank of 'Boy Regimental Sergeant Major'. It looked very promising until he clashed with the real RSM. The reason is unknown, but it resulted in Jack and a friend going AWOL (Absent without leave). The two were on the run for a few weeks until apprehended and returned to camp. The outcome was Jack being discharged from boy service but with no stain on his character.

On reaching the age of eighteen he was called into the Army for National Service and joined the Royal Army Medical Corps. He did not like the RAMC and immediately asked for a transfer to the Royal Army Service Corps where a year later he was to meet his future wife, Marian Alexander Cawley. He was serving in 21 Company RASC and Marian in 70 Company Women's Royal Army Corps, both based at Hounslow in Middlesex. Jack spent most of his time in the Army driving 'Matador' transport vehicles hauling coastal guns of the Royal Artillery up and down the east coast of England.

Jack and Marian were married in Ealing in 1956 in the county of Middlesex and their son Kevin was born in 1957. The marriage did not last long before they divorced and went their own way. An unfounded story was that Marian was already married but this was never substantiated. Jack left the Army on completion of his National Service commitment and for a while, he teamed up with our brother George working on construction sites around Yorkshire.

He decided to branch out on his own and took a course in salesmanship at which he excelled, and soon became an instructor in selling. He then started a small business selling and repairing vacuum cleaners. He rented a shop in Thornton Street Hull and took on four girls, part-time, to tour the houses of the area drumming up business. Jack's partner during this time was Sheila Duffield* and they had three daughters, Sandra, Susan, Mandy, and a son, Paul. At the same time, Jack had custody of Kevin, his son from his marriage to Marian Cawley.

Whilst enjoying the nightclub life in Hull, he met his second wife to be, Vivienne (nee Gray) from Beverley in Yorkshire who was working in one of the clubs frequented by Jack. For some unknown reason his business had collapsed, and he had separated from his partner Sheila. Jack married Vivienne in 1963 and they had a daughter, Vivienne and a son Martin. They rented a house in Hull, but the marriage soon hit trouble and there was a great deal of friction between the two of them. Jack had become involved with a group of men who had plans to set up a 'protection racket' in the city of Hull. Jack was a major player and it was his intention to be the boss.

The plan got off to a bad start when the first potential victim of the racket informed the police, which resulted in the gang being arrested. After a five-day trial at the Hull Crown Court, various lengths of prison sentences were given to each member. Jack had by then already committed suicide, but in his absence, he was mentioned at every stage of the trial. He had been told, wrongly, by his lawyer that he was likely to be given a lengthy custodial sentence as he had already been in prison on two occasions for non-payment of child maintenance. No one in the family was aware of his intentions but assumed he was afraid of going back to prison for a lengthy period.

In October 1971, after visiting every member of the Lockwood and Gray family still living in Withernsea he drove his car to the cliff edge of the small coastal village of Tunstall, three miles from Withernsea, and ended his life by fitting a tube from the engine of the car, sealing the windows, and with the engine running, dying from carbon monoxide poisoning. He had sent his wife Vivienne a letter prior to his suicide but whatever reason he gave for taking his own life was never revealed to the family and the letter was burnt. Vivienne met and married David Holwell sometime after Jack's death and the surname of Jack's two children, Martin, and Vivienne, were changed to that of their stepfather.

* After Jack and Sheila parted, Sheila had one more daughter, Andria, who married Lee Farmer, and was a half-sister to Jack and Sheila's family.

Vivienne and David set up a family-run garden centre business in Hollym, a few miles from Withernsea, and for many years produced a variety of garden ornaments and became well known for the quality of their products. They also had a fish farm, breeding 'Japanese Koi' a popular decorative pond fish. Business was good and flourished and when Vivienne and David retired and moved to Vivienne's birthplace Beverley, they left Martin to run the workshop and aquarium. After a few years, even though it was still a successful enterprise the lack of labour to help with the heavy lifting of the concrete products became too much for Martin on his own and had, reluctantly, to close the business down. Vivienne passed away in February 2016 and David continued to live in Beverley where they had retired to a few years earlier.

Martin and his partner Katrina Jayne Whincup had two children: Adam Charles and Abbie Rose. His sister Vivienne enjoyed a spell of moved to North Yorkshire where she met and married David Barber. They had two children David and John. Martin married Rebecca Hymus and they had a son George born in 2007. They continue to live in the same house in Hollym from which the garden centre business had originally been formed.

James Kenneth

1939 -

As a baby Jim, as we all called him, was the darling of the family. He immediately became the favourite of June and Alice and they would take it in turn to look after him. He grew up with a very docile temperament always smiling and laughing, loved by everyone and during our stay in Withernsea he was just as adventurous as the rest of us. When we parted at Patrington I was not to see him again for about four years when we met together sometime after the war had ended. All the children of the homes in East Yorkshire were brought together for a seven-day holiday in Withernsea.

The accommodation was the classrooms of the modern High School, which had a huge playing field that was ideal for so many children to play cricket, football and enjoy normal children's games. He had been transferred from Driffield to Cottingham with Jack and Freda and as with them, he was not happy in his new home. After I left the home Jim disappeared from my life again and it was at one of June's daughter's wedding that I caught up with him again and we have been close ever since.

He recently told me about the problems he had with Miss Duncumb. As he grew older, he became more outspoken and rebellious with the result that he became the target of Miss Duncumb's fiery temper. He ran away from the house on several occasions but was always caught and returned. After his last attempt he was being viciously caned by Miss Duncumb when he called her a' big fat pig' At that she went berserk, and as Jim recalled, she bounced him off all the walls in the kitchen, kicking and punching him. She then dragged him upstairs and locked in a cupboard in the isolation room for the rest of the day and all the night. No food or water was provided and the next morning he had to sit on a chair in the kitchen, naked, whilst the other children had to watch and were warned this is what happens if they did not behave. That same morning a car arrived, and both Jim and Freda were taken to separate homes, Jim to Sigglesthorne, a small village near Beverley and Freda to a foster home into the care of Mrs. Dorsey until she reached the age of eighteen.

It was to be many years before they were to see each other again. He completed a plumbing apprenticeship and was immediately called up for his National Service and volunteered for the Royal Navy. He signed on for nine years and after training joined his first ship, the Frigate H.M.S. Ulysses and on completion of the ship's world tour, he volunteered for submarine service. His first boat was H.M. Submarine 'Tapir' followed three years later by 'Totem'. It was whilst serving on this boat a life-changing event occurred that would determine his and his family path for the rest of their lives.

The submarine and crew were posted to Balmoral Naval Base in Sydney Australia for two years. He became attracted to the Australian way of life and decided he would leave the Navy on his return to England and emigrate with his family. He had married Wendy Silman in Todmorden where they had two boys: Terry and James. He had no difficulty in finding work and was soon a foreman working on the prestigious 'Sydney Opera House' supervising a section installing the air conditioning system. Wendy had also found work in an office and the boys entered the Australian way of life swimming, surfing, and playing rugby. When the work ended, he formed his own air conditioning business in Sydney and soon became a well-known and respected businessman.

Work was plentiful and when he retired at the age of sixty, he owned two properties, one in the Sydney suburbs and the second, a holiday home further down the coast about thirty miles from Sydney. Jim and Wendy decided they would sell both properties and move to the township of Urunga situated on the coast about five-hundred miles north of the New South Wales capital. Here they were to spend the remainder of their lives in a very pleasant part of NSW in a house with a three-acre garden, surrounded by farmland, close to the sea and with a fishing river almost on their doorstep.

For a few year's life was good to both but one of their sons, Terrance, became involved with the surfing fraternity living a wayward life which was to give both his parents many problems. James, their second son, had married Narelle, an Australian girl, and lived in Sydney, they had one son and two daughters. Life for Jim and Wendy took a downward turn when Wendy became increasingly ill with a respiratory illness, partly due to smoking and her earlier teenage years working in the cotton mills in her hometown of Todmorden. After a long struggle against cancer, she passed away in 2016. Jim continues to live in Urunga indulging in his passion for fishing in the nearby sea and rivers that run close to his property.

Eveline Freda Gray
1942

Freda grew up never meeting her father and for most of her childhood saw extraordinarily little of her mother. During her early life, she only lived with her mother for a total of twenty-one months and never again in her lifetime. Taken into care in June 1944 she was placed in a children's home in Driffield, a small market town fifteen miles north of Hull. With two of her brothers, Jim, and Jack they lived a good happy life until they were transferred from Driffield to Cottingham sometime between 1949 and 1950. It was not to be a happy move for any of them. Freda was the youngest of the twelve children in the Cottingham home with a matron who had no experience of looking after girls and one so young as Freda. No allowance was made for her age and she was treated just the same as anyone else. Her worst experience was breakfast. Every morning she had to sit at the table and eat her three slices of bread and dripping just the same as the others. She had been taken from a happy relaxed home and thrust into a hostile environment.

In May 1952, after an incident between Jim and Miss Duncumb, she was removed from Cottingham and taken into care by Mrs Dorsey who lived in the small market town of Pocklington. Cruelly Freda was parted from her brother Jim, the only one she had spent the whole of her life with. Jim was taken to a new home ten miles away in the village of Sigglesthorne without either of them knowing where the other had gone. At the tender age of nine years old she had been in three different homes after the family broke up in 1944. From the workhouse to Driffield, then to Cottingham and finally to Pocklington.

From the age of fifteen when she left school in 1957, she first took up employment with Terry and Sons Ltd York for a weekly wage of £2,16 shillings and sixpence. Later, in 1958, she took up employment as an office girl with M. Hartland & Sons, Printers in Pocklington .On reaching the age of eighteen Freda enlisted into the Women's Royal Army Corps and it was whilst serving with this unit she met and eventually married her husband Alan Charlton who was serving his National Service commitment. After their discharge from the Army, they set up home in Alan's hometown of Middlesbrough on Tees-Side. Here they raised their family of one girl, Jane, and three boys, Alan, Stephen, and Michael.

After I left the home, it was the last time I was to see Freda for ten years. When we did meet again, we didn't know each other. I passed her in the passage of June's house as I was arriving one day, and she was leaving. I asked June who that person in uniform was just going out the door and she said, 'that was your sister Freda'. I didn't see her for a long time after that, and I can't remember how we came to meet again or where. We are now close friends and see each other on a regular basis

Freda & Alan

Part Three

Chapter 7

The Lockwood family

My mother was the youngest of three daughters of John and Sarah Lockwood. She suffered a life-changing accident when she was about three years old when her nightdress caught fire when looking up the chimney for Father Christmas. Her burns were so severe she was transferred to a specialist burns hospital in London. In those early years, the treatment of burns was not as technically advanced as they are today and she was to suffer severe pain, the memory of which still haunted her into her late years. The accident was the start of many years of painful treatment followed by difficult years learning how to do things with her left hand rather than her deformed right hand. The scars on her lower face, chest, arms, and hands stayed with her for the remainder of her life. She had no formal education, resulting in having to take low paid work as a scullery maid in the home of a wealthy family in Kingston, Surrey.

At the age of nineteen, she became pregnant and she has always insisted that the father of her daughter, June Elizabeth, was a member of the family she worked for. Three weeks after the birth, my mother with her newborn daughter was put on a train back to Hull which she had left sixteen years previously. It can only be assumed she went back to live with her parents. There is no family history of her movements in the following years or how she came to meet George Frederick Gray, but she became his 'common-law wife' sometime between 1928 and 1930. Her sister Norah told the story that they did plan to marry but one of my father's sisters turned up at their house insisting they could not marry, as he was already married and had a son. The story could not be substantiated but an official record for the district does show him being married and my mother as a single woman so there could have been some truth in the story.

With her second family of three boys and one girl, her life of struggle and poverty continued, but by then the welfare system had reduced the scale of poverty quite considerably compared with the 2nd World War years. School attendance for her family improved and with the return to civilian life of many of the male teachers, the discipline also improved. Gradually life became much better for my mother and she was able to move from Queen Street to better accommodation on a nearby housing estate.

Whilst her family had been making their way in life, mam had been doing what all grandmothers do, looking after the grandchildren. She was never free of children until they were either in school or had started working for a living. At last, she could start having a life of her own even to travelling down to Hampshire with June to stay with Betty and me. On two separate visits, we took her to Wembley Stadium to watch the massed bands of the British Army in their spectacular bi-yearly band shows. The speed of the Light Infantry, the skirl of the pipes, and the colour of the uniforms and the whole atmosphere of the fifty thousand spectators mesmerized her. It was a whole new experience and one she would never forget. She was also able to travel to Todmorden in Yorkshire to attend the wedding of my brother Jim to Wendy Silman. Although she was never confident enough to make journeys on her own, she always had her eldest daughter June for company. Occasionally, Michael and Sandra would take her for a holiday to Whitby, a popular holiday town on the North Yorkshire coast which she enjoyed tremendously.

From her early childhood accident, her life had been one of pain from her burns, a difficult rehabilitation, drudgery as a scullery maid, sexual abuse at an early age, beaten by her drunken common-law-husband, forty years of childbearing, and abject poverty for most of her life. She finally had a house that could be called a 'home'. Tom had provided one of his properties for her to live in and the remainder of the Lockwood family rallied round with regular visits to make sure she wanted for nothing. Constant improvements in welfare and living conditions gradually lifted the poverty my mother had endured for most of her life and after a few years moved into a 'warden controlled' bungalow for the rest of her life.

Of the Lockwood family, there were three boys: Michael, Tom, Graham, and a daughter Sandra. With regular attendance at school it gave the family a far better chance of making a good living and they made full use of what was on offer. As young boys, Michael and Tom took on any work to earn money, most of which they gave to mam in return for a small amount for ice cream, cinema, etc. One of the most popular, but hardest, was as 'barrow boys'. In the summer months when the holidaymakers arrived in Withernsea they would carry the bags and cases of the arrivals and take them to the various caravan sites on the outskirts of Withernsea. This was heavy and tiring work as the main sites were at least a mile from the station. They didn't have a set price for their demanding work, so they had to depend on the generosity of the customer and occasionally it was hardly worth the effort.

In the early sixties, a photograph was taken by an unknown photographer of a group of boys waiting at the railway station to carry the luggage of incoming holidaymakers. They had made the barrows from old boxes and pram wheels, no longer used for their original purpose. The photograph was to become one of the Iconic photographs of the early sixties in Withernsea. It shows seven boys (Tom and Michael bottom left) totally absorbed in a remark in what the boy on the extreme right had said. The expressions on their faces have been captured and show the innocence and happiness of childhood.

Collecting empty bottles was also another activity that could produce a small sum of cash. They would scour the caravan sites and the beach area looking for empty bottles to return them to their original source. The standard price for a bottle was a penny and at that time there were two hundred and forty pence to one pound. One of the hardest jobs was potato picking in the summer months. As well as being paid a decent wage there was a bonus for this backbreaking job, a bag of potatoes, which would be stored in the alcove of the middle room at home. They were never hungry, but as Tom once remarked they almost looked like 'chips' having eaten so many potatoes. Delivering newspapers, both in the morning and evenings, easy in the summer months but much harder in the winter.

During the winter they would also deliver coke to people in the north end of Withernsea and this was done using a worn-out pram or improvised barrow. Always looking to earn extra money they worked on farms harvesting wheat and barley. Tom also had a job packing eggs and general maintenance work on a chicken farm. One job he did not like was wading in the 'sully pit 'underneath the cages in chest waders looking up at the cages for dead chickens. It was a two-man job with Tom in the pit indicating to the person above, with a bamboo stick, where there were any dead chickens, which had to be removed. Very often the dead birds would fall apart creating a horrendous smell. Unpleasant work but it was a way to make money. At Christmas time Michael and Tom even resorted to Christmas carol singing but very often their efforts were not appreciated and were told plainly to 'clear off'.

Tom, Sandra, Mam, Michael, and Graham

Michael

Michael was born in the same bed as the earlier four children of mam's second family in 24 Queens Street, Withernsea, a house with no indoor facilities or even carpets on the floor. Heating was by coal fires in the kitchen, middle room, and front room where the bed was situated. In later years a bathroom was added, and the house wired up for electricity.

As a young boy, Michael took a newspaper round delivering papers seven days a week. He also collected and delivered cinders (coke) from the local gas works during the winter months and was one of the barrow boys during the summer months. At the age of fourteen, he took a job working on a threshing machine and, using a winding machine, transported sacks of beans and corn weighing from twelve to twenty-two stone up to the granary. For this extremely challenging work, he was paid twenty-one shillings a day. No doubt the hard-physical work was good preparation for his love of Rugby Union which he was to become a very good player for Withernsea High School. and later for Withernsea R.U.F.C. of which he was captain at the age of sixteen. He then moved on to play for 'Old Hymerians' one of the top teams in the Yorkshire league. He was made captain of the team at the age of thirty-six before moving to the 'veterans' and retired from the game at the age of fifty.

Michael had worked hard at school and with encouragement from one of his teachers he became interested in design and drawing, which he put to effective use, designing private, and commercial buildings for various clients in the East Riding of Yorkshire and further afield. He soon branched out into designing houses and eventually, in later years, building them on his own sites. He met Sandra Harrison on a blind date in 1963 and they married in 1970. They had a son Andrew and a daughter Clare. Clare was born with additional needs and would require constant attention throughout her life. Michael promised that Clare would never go into a care home and would be looked after by her own family. To the credit of Michael and Sandra, she has had all the love and attention given so that she could lead an as normal life as possible. He designed and built a house for her to facilitate the necessary equipment to make life as easy as possible for both Clare and her parents. Michael, Sandra, and Clare moved from their home of forty years to a newly built Dormer Bungalow, designed by Michael only a few yards from their old home.

He made a career as a draftsman working from his home in Roos, a house which he had completely rebuilt from the inside to his own design and he lived there with his wife and family for forty years. In addition to his designing and building work, he bought a few vacant properties in Withernsea, building an impressive property portfolio. Their son Andrew married Kerry Oxlade, the wedding taking place on the beach in Australia. They had a son Joe Harrison and a daughter, Francesca Grace but the marriage was not to last and after a few years, they divorced

Sandra and Michael

Sandra

Whilst her brothers were earning money to help the family finances, Sandra was also doing her bit. Before she left school, she worked in the 'Redferns' café on the promenade and looked after her youngest brother Graham whilst mam was also able to go out to work. After leaving school she took a job in Redferns crisp factory in Patrington in what was, the old workhouse before it was closed and where mam and five of her first family were separated June 1944. Sandra was employed at Withernsea High school as a cleaner and then for a good few years at the Pavilion and Leisure Centre. She also worked as a lithographer at the Withernsea Potteries adding paintings of woodland creatures to the company's products.

Sandra met her future husband Dave Lockwood, (not related to our Lockwood family), who worked in the office of the Parks department in Hull. David played rugby for the same Withernsea team as her brother Michael and that is how they met. Sandra and David married in 1976 and raised three sons, Paul, Mark, and Darren.

Sadly, Sandra died in August 2008 after a brave fight against cancer. She would have been enormously proud of her three sons and the successful lives they each achieved.

The wedding of Sandra and David

Paul

Paul, the eldest son, studied for a sports science degree at Hull Riley Centre and did a 'master's in business's and integrated leisure management accredited through Hull University. Before that, he gained a diploma from the Institute of sport and leisure management (ISRM) accredited through Loughborough University. He has worked for East Riding Leisure since 1995 in numerous roles from Leisure Management, Business Commissioning and now Healthy Lifestyles Development Manager in conjunction with Public Health and the ER Clinical Commissioning Group. He married Rachael Kirby who formed her own successful business after taking a degree in 'Sports Therapy'. She has her own business in physiotherapy and owns the East Yorkshire Therapy Clinic.

Darren

Daren trained in the print industry, starting at ITec in Hull and gained an NVQ in 'pre-press'. He now works for a Flexographic printing company which specialises in flexible food packaging. He continues to live with his father David at home in Withernsea.

Mark

Mark took 'A levels in Maths, Physics, and Computing' at Wilberforce College in Hull. In 1999 he started his 'Deck Officer Cadetship' with 'Maersk-line'. His time was split between time served on Maersk tanker and container vessels and studying at Glasgow Nautical College. One of his completed projects during this time was awarded a prize, which was presented to him by Princess Anne on behalf of the Marine Society. In 2003 he completed his Cadetship passing his 'Officer of The Watch Certificate of Competency' at the MCA office in Greenock. He then sailed with Maersk on worldwide trades as 4th, 3rd, and 2nd officer. In late 2006 he sat his exams for a 'Chief Officer Certificate of Competency' and was successful. Whilst studying for these exams his mother, Sandra, fell seriously ill and Mark decided he could not continue with long deep-sea trips and applied for a post with the 'Scottish Fisheries Protection Agency' (now Marine Scotland). He was recruited as 2nd Officer in early 2007. In 2008 he was sailing as Chief Officer and successfully passed his 'Master Mariner' ticket in 2010. In 2013 was promoted to Captain on the company's newest vessel, the 'HIRTA' at the age of 32. In 2017 he was promoted again to 'Marine Superintendent' to manage the company fleet from shore side. Mark married Leanne who is a primary school teacher and they now live permanently in Scotland with their two children, Cole and Calla.

David Lockwood, Paul, Rachel, Darren, Leanne with Cole, and Mark.

Tom

From Withernsea High School Tom graduated to the Hull Nautical College, the premier establishment in England and the oldest in the world, for the training of Sea Cadets for service in the Merchant Marine. He failed on his first application but was successful on his second attempt. He confessed he was not accepted on his academic qualifications, but that 'God' loves a trier.

Coming from a one-parent family it was financially difficult and embarrassing when most of the other cadets came from a higher class of society. One embarrassing incident for Tom was during a Macintosh parade when every cadet had to bring his coat for inspection. This was two years after he had joined the school and still could not afford to buy one. He admitted it was not the cold that worried him but the embarrassment of not having the money to buy one and the headmaster not being able to understand why he did not have enough funds. Boys from poor backgrounds were very rare in that type of establishment and Tom stood out like a sore thumb.

Further financial embarrassment occurred when he left the school and was ordered to report to his first ship, 'MV Olivebank'. He received a list of the clothing and books he would need for the voyage and was horrified when he saw how much it was to cost, about £60, and with no possibility of any help from the family, the dream of becoming a 'nautical navigation cadet' began to evaporate. Fortunately, the family of one of Tom's friends came to his rescue and loaned him the necessary fund to buy his kit. He went to sea owing £60 on a weekly wage of £3. He sent £1 home to his mother and the rest to pay off his debt.

After a while, he gave up his apprenticeship and joined the fishing fleet for two years including Arctic trawlers. He soon realized the fishing fleet was under pressure and would not be long before it went to the wall and rejoined the Merchant Navy. For five years he served as a deckhand before returning to the nautical college to take his Coastal Navigation certificate. He failed his first attempt but cleared the hurdle on the second time around. Two years later he again returned to Hull Nautical College to take his 'Master's Coastal Certificate' which he passed at the first attempt. The result came on the same day he passed his driving test at the fifth attempt.

He continued to work on ships tramping the world for a good many year. Tom married Helen Stevenson in 1980 and they had two children, Christopher, and Gemma. Tom decided to find work ashore and took an eight-month plumbing course at 'City & Guilds' level and on to advanced level passing with a distinction.

To gain the experience he took a job on a farm doing the plumbing and building work in addition to looking after the pigs and other farm animals. At the same time, he had started a small mini skip business, which lasted about two years and settled in Withernsea, buying and renovating houses, and building fishing ponds. He acquired a few properties to rent out, building an impressive property portfolio. Tom and Helen have four grandchildren: Thomas Wynn Lockwood-Davies and Ruby Ellen Lockwood-Davies. Christopher and his partner Tara have two children, Anna Rose, and Georgia Sophia. Chris, at the age of thirty-four, and Tara are also building a sizable property portfolio in Withernsea.

Tom returned to the merchant navy in 1997 after re-validating and updating his certificates. He joined a small deep-sea tug company out of Lowestoft doing ocean towage, rig moves, and salvage work. He stayed with the company for almost thirteen years until retiring in 2010 at the age of sixty. Tom had sailed the world for several years diligently saving his money to buy plots of land on which he could develop and build fishing ponds. Gradually he increased the size of the ponds until in 2001 he bought a three-acre plot on which he built a two-acre pond with a magnificent house for the family, and in addition, he also acquired a few properties in Withernsea to rent out. Two of the Lockwood family had made it out of poverty to being landlords and landowners!!

The fishing pond built by Tom

Graham

Graham did not have the ambition or drive of his older brothers. After leaving school his main employment was farm work, mainly working with pigs and other animals. Due to the number of fertilizers, pesticides, and dust from animal feeds it all amounted to an unhealthy occupation resulting in a deterioration of his health which resulted in him having to give up farm work. He started work as a security officer in one of the large retail stores in the city of Hull. His health did improve but most of the damage had already been done, which was to seriously affect him in later years. He married June McCranor in 1978 and they had four daughters: Sharon, Rebecca, Naomi, and Natasha. Sadly, Natasha developed a serious illness and passed away in 2003 at the age of seventeen. A very much-loved daughter and sister.

Graham and June were well known in their village for the spectacular Christmas Lights display every year which not only gave his own family a great deal of pleasure but also his neighbours and the local population of their village. Sharon, the eldest of the four girls attended Hull University for three years and gained a degree in nursing. After several years in local medical establishments, she went on to York Teaching Hospital, leaving Withernsea to live in the beautiful Yorkshire Dales with her partner Clint Eastwood and their daughters Courtney and Lauren. Graham's other daughters; Naomi and Rebecca both became 'Carers' and continue to live in Withernsea close to their partners and families.

June and Graham's wedding

Chapter 8
George Frederick Gray
1897 - 1970

My father was born in 1897 to Sarah Ann Gray in the coastal town of Bridlington, East Yorkshire. He was illegitimate, as were his two sisters: Annie Eliza b 1881 and Lotty b 1884. When he reached the age of fifteen, he was enlisted into the Army as a boy musician for the mandatory term of twelve years with the Border Regiment. On reaching the age of eighteen on 3rd September 1915 he was posted to the ranks, first to the 3rd Battalion and then the 7th Battalion. In 1918 he took part in the last few months of the Second Battle of the Somme and suffered a gunshot wound to his right thigh*. He excelled in sport including, boxing, football, hockey, and tug of war, and in 1918 he was in the winning regimental tug of war team that won the Southern Area championships.

In 1921 the regiment was posted to India for a three-year tour and during that period the battalion was engaged in operations against the rebels in Waziristan on the NW Frontier, the notorious mountainous area that included the Khyber Pass, controlled by the fearsome Afghan rebels. Whilst in India his twelve-year engagement came to an end and he opted for discharge, which he took on the homeward journey during a stopover in Aden. His disciplinary report was not good, drink and lack of respect for his superiors was a bad omen for his future employment prospects. He was sentenced to twenty-eight days detention for being absent without permission and a further ninety days whilst in Aden for drunkenness and striking a superior officer.

In 1939 he was recalled to the Army and as he was not eligible for the infantry because of his age he was posted to the newly formed Auxiliary Pioneer Corps. This corps absorbed all those former soldiers who were too old for the fighting regiments and were to be used for any type of labour required to keep the front-line troops supplied with all the ammunition, food, stores, weapons, and general paraphernalia of war. He served in Malta, North Africa, and Austria picking up a few more detentions for being drunk and absent from his place of duty. Three times he was reduced in rank, once from sergeant and twice from corporal. His character assessment on discharge from the Army in 1945 read simply 'BAD'.

On leaving the Army he settled in Hull but did not make any contact with my mother or any of his children. He simply deserted his responsibilities and took up with another partner by the name of Ivy Winterbottom. Without any skills, he could only find employment as a general labourer, first on the building sites around Hull and then on a tunnel project where he spent time as a 'bookies runner' and general 'dogs' body.

George, Jack, Jim and I did see him again in about 1966 long after the war had finished but by then he showed little interest in the family he had deserted almost twelve years previously. I saw him walking along New Village Road in Hull and I stopped him to say hello. He was pleased to see me and invited me to his house for Sunday dinner where I met his present partner Ivy. He did ask how our mother was and where the others of the family were living. From then on, we would go to see him, but it was always in his local pub where he could be found any day along with his mates from his army days and newfound friends in the Alexandra pub close to where he lived. The last time I saw him he was lying in a hospital bed with scalp wounds, the result of a fight in a pub with a much younger man who had knocked him down and then kicked his head, causing considerable damage. My younger brother Jack soon heard about the incident and paid the young man a visit and went ahead to settle the score in the 'time-honored way'. He died in 1970 and was cremated in the Hull crematorium with only June, George, Jack, and me in attendance. If ever a man wasted his life it was him. Without a father to guide him and teach responsibility, he spent most of his time pursuing his own pleasures without any thought to the family he had created fifty years previously.

* There is every possibility that the weakness in his right leg which prevented him from taking up a career as a professional footballer was the result of the wound suffered during the war.

1.British War Medal. 2. Victory Medal. 3. Indian GSM Clasp Waziristan.
4. 1939-45 Star. 5. Italy Star. 6. Defense Medal. 7. War Medal 1939-1944

Epilogue

By the year 2017, only three members of the original Gray family of 1930 were still living. Jim was in Australia; Freda in Middlesbrough and I was living in the Hampshire town of Fleet. Both our parents had died of heart disease, June and Sally succumbed to cancer, George to dementia and Jack had taken his own life. Three of the original Lockwood family were still in Withernsea, Sandra having passed away in August 2008. During the intervening eighty-seven years there have been over one hundred and thirty descendants of both families. It had been seventy-seven years since the Gray family broke up in Withernsea, never to live as a family again. Jim, Freda, and I had not been together since I left the Children's home in 1950. I had seen Jim on two occasions (once in Australia) and Freda regularly after I left the Army, but the three of us had not been together since our parting in Cottingham. We came together during a family reunion, ironically in Withernsea, the town where we last lived together as a family unit in 1944. The reunion was held over a three-day period 8th-10th September 2017. During the weekend fifty family members came together, meeting half brothers and sisters they did not know they had, and others they had not seen for many years. It was an enormous success, an event that our mam would have enjoyed so much seeing that many of her family all in one place.

Jim Freda and Fred together for the first time in sixty-seven years

Some of the family who attended the first reunion in 2017

And again in 2018

The Gray's

James Kenneth

Jack (John)

Frederick William

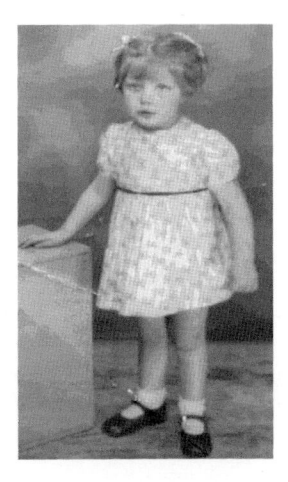

Freda (Eveline)

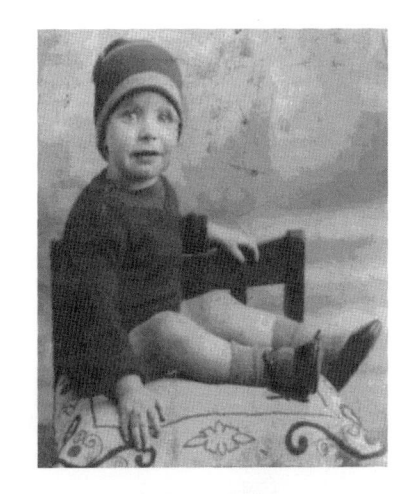

George William

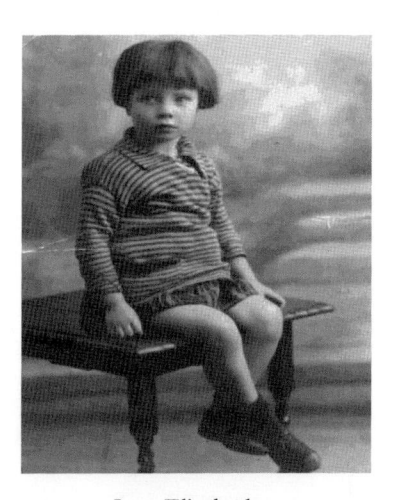

June Elizabeth

James Kenneth

Sally

June Elizabeth

Sally and George

The Lockwood Family

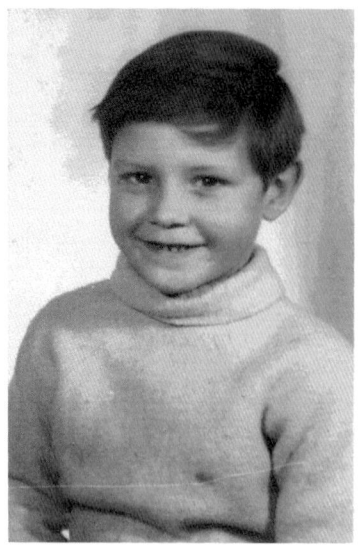

Graham

Tommy

Michael

Sandra

When you mentioned the senna pods I shuddered as other memories came to me. I wasn't a big eater, I'm still skinny (wiry my daughter teases!) and often I couldn't finish a meal. It was served up time and time again until I did eat it. This would end with me being physically sick and I would be made to eat that as well. I wasn't the only one either — several children suffered the same penalties. I was in the home

An original letter sent to the author, by one of the children many years later.

Printed in Great
Britain
by Amazon